The YOUR STEPS TOWARD SUCCESS *Career Resource Workbook will be my guide and platform for my future.*

Gerardo Garcia
The University of Texas at El Paso
El Paso, Texas
(University Student)

My YOUR STEPS TOWARD SUCCESS *Career Resource Workbook is never far from me. I use this tool more than I do any other reference book...you will too.*

Angela Watson
Mississippi Delta Epsilon Chi State Chairperson
Baldwyn, Mississippi
(Job Seeker)

I find the YOUR STEPS TOWARD SUCCESS *Career Resource Workbook the most informative book I have ever read.*

Stephen Morely
McIntosh College
Dover, New Hampshire
(Non-Traditional College Student)

Every student and job seekers must utilize the YOUR STEPS TOWARD SUCCESS *Career Resource Workbook, which contains great activities designed to further develop an individual's employability skills. Having personally used the* YOUR STEPS TOWARD SUCCESS *Career Resource Workbook at several conferences, I have witnessed how the student attendees left the conference better prepared to achieve their career goals. When they returned to their campus, their leadership abilities shone and were noticed by other educators and administrators.*

Jack J. Rose
Professor
Johnson & Wales University
Florida Campus
and
Executive Director
Florida Delta Epsilon Chi
Plantation, Florida

CAREER RESOURCE WORKBOOK

YOUR
STEPS
TOWARD
SUCCESS

ANGELA DAYTON, M.S.

Bloomington, IN Milton Keynes, UK

authorHOUSE

AuthorHouse™
1663 Liberty Drive, Suite 200
Bloomington, IN 47403
www.authorhouse.com
Phone: 1-800-839-8640

AuthorHouse™ UK Ltd.
500 Avebury Boulevard
Central Milton Keynes, MK9 2BE
www.authorhouse.co.uk
Phone: 08001974150

ISBN: 1-4259-2378-X (sc)

First published by AuthorHouse 03/20/2007

Printed in the United States of America
Bloomington, Indiana

This book is printed on acid-free paper.

Disclaimer: The purpose of this book is to educate. The author or publisher does not guarantee that anyone following the ideas, tips, suggestions, techniques or strategies will become successful. The author and publisher shall have neither liability nor responsibility to anyone with respect to any loss or damage caused, or alleged to be caused, directly or indirectly by the information contained in this book.

Contents

CHOOSING YOUR CAREER

LANDING THE JOB YOU WANT

ADVANCING IN YOUR CAREER

LEADING YOUR TEAM TO SUCCESS

CHOOSING YOUR CAREER

Occupational Choices

Purpose

The purpose of this lesson is to discuss tools that will help you become educated about your career choices.

Objectives

Check each objective upon completion.

- ❏ Conduct a self-analysis.

- ❏ Identify the high growth industries.

- ❏ List the available research tools.

- ❏ Conduct research on interesting industries and occupations.

Conducting a Self-Analysis

To begin your journey, you need to conduct a self-analysis. Set time aside to think about your preferences, your motivations, your goals, and your future.

What is important to you in a career?

_____

_____

_____

What motivates you?

_____

_____

_____

What are your hobbies?

_____

_____

_____

What qualities do you have?

_____

_____

_____

What are your strengths?

_____

_____

_____

What are your weaknesses?

_____

_____

_____

Do you prefer working with others or by yourself? Why?

_____

_____

_____

Who are you? Describe yourself.

_____

_____

_____

What are your career goals?

_____

_____

_____

What would you like to be doing five years from now?

_____

_____

_____

How do you define success?

_____

_____

_____

What kind of work are you most interested in?

_____

_____

_____

What types of positions are you interested in?

_____

_____

_____

What do you expect from your career?

_____

_____

_____

What were/are your favorite classes/activities in school? Why?

_____

_____

_____

How many years do you want to devote to school/training?

_____

_____

_____

Researching Occupations in High Growth Industries

Now that you have a better idea of your preferences, you can begin researching potential careers by using the following guidelines:

- Determine if the occupation will be in demand when you graduate from school or finish your training
- Research the occupational skills and educational/training requirements
- Conduct informational interviews with individuals who are working in the field
- Shadow individuals who are working in the field
- Complete an internship

Occupational Demand

There are numerous research groups that publish information on careers. When conducting your research, use multiple resources, such as the U.S. Bureau of Labor Statistics, Economy.com, U.S. Bureau of Economic Analysis, Hoover's Online, America's Career InfoNet, industry publications, job banks, etc.

During your research, you will want to note the growth patterns of the industries and the occupational outlooks for the specific careers you are interested in pursuing.

For example, the following information communicates the growth pattern of the biotechnology industry. These are the types of facts you would want to identify if you were pursuing an occupation within the biotechnology industry:

- The biotechnology industry has more than tripled in size since 1992, and revenues increased from $8 billion in 1992 to $27.6 billion in 2001.[1]

- Most occupations in the biotechnology industry require a 2-year, 4-year, or more advanced education.[2]

- The population of companies engaged in biotechnology is dynamic and growth in the biotechnology-related workforce has been vigorous, averaging 12.3 percent annually for those companies that provided data for 2000-2002. Companies with 50 to 499 employees experienced the fastest growth, with an annual increase of 17.3 percent, while growth among larger firms was 6.2 percent.[3]

- The biotechnology industry employed 713,000 workers in 2002 and is anticipated to employ 814,900 workers in 2007.[4]

- Employment in pharmaceutical and medical manufacturing is projected to increase from 293,000 to 361,000 jobs during 2002 to 2012, representing an increase of 68,000 jobs and an average annual rate of change of 2.1 percent.[5]

- The occupation of biological technician is expected to grow by 19.4 percent between 2002 and 2012, while the occupation of biological scientist is projected to grow by 19.0 percent.[6]

- Computer specialists in the life sciences are among the high-technology employment categories currently experiencing job growth.[7]

The occupational outlook for the biotechnology industry is as follows:

Occupation Title	Number Employed 2002 (000s)	Number Employed 2012 (000s)	Numeric Change (000s)	Change %	2002 Median Annual Earnings	Postsecondary Education & Training
Medical scientists, except epidemiologists	58	73	16	26.9	56,980	Doctorate degree
Biomedical engineers	8	10	2	26.1	60,410	Bachelor's degree
Environmental scientists and specialists, including health	65	80	15	23.7	47,600	Master's degree
Biological scientists, all other	27	33	6	22.3	53,300	Bachelor's degree
Biological technicians	48	57	9	19.4	29,040	Associate's degree
Chemists	84	95	11	12.7	52,890	Bachelor's degree
Agricultural & food science technicians	20	22	2	9.3	28,580	Associate's degree
Chemical technicians	69	72	3	4.7	37,430	Bachelor's degree

Source: U.S. Bureau of Labor Statistics / 000s represent thousands

High Growth Industries

The U.S. Department of Labor's Employment and Training Administration has identified 15 high growth industries at the national level. The identified industries:

1. are projected to add substantial numbers of new jobs to the economy;
2. have a significant impact on the overall U.S. economy;
3. impact the growth of other industries;
4. are being transformed by technology and innovation requiring new skill sets for workers; and/or
5. are new and emerging businesses that are projected to grow.

The high growth industries are:
- Advanced Manufacturing
- Aerospace
- Automotive Services
- Biotechnology
- Construction
- Energy
- Financial Services
- Geospatial Technology
- Health Care
- Hospitality
- Information Technology
- Nanotechnology
- Public Safety
- Retail Trade
- Transportation

You will want to choose an occupation that is within a high growth industry and has a positive growth pattern.

Determining Occupational Knowledge, Skills and Abilities

As you are researching your chosen occupation, you should be identifying the knowledge, skills, and abilities you will need to achieve success in your career. The details of an occupation can be found by using a variety of sources, such as America's Career InfoNet, Occupational Information Network (O*Net), Career Voyages, industry associations, job banks, U.S. Bureau of Labor Statistics' Occupational Outlook Handbook, and other resources.

The following is an example of the research you would find for the Biological Technician occupation within the biotechnology industry. According to America's Career InfoNet[8] the most important knowledge, skills, and abilities for Biological Technicians are as follows:

Knowledge:

- *Chemistry* - Knowledge of the chemical composition, structure, and properties of substances and of the chemical processes and transformations that they undergo. This includes uses of chemicals and their interactions, danger signs, production techniques, and disposal methods.

- *Biology* - Knowledge of plant and animal organisms, their tissues, cells, functions, interdependencies, and interactions with each other and the environment.

- *Mathematics* - Knowledge of arithmetic, algebra, geometry, calculus, statistics, and their applications.

- *English Language* - Knowledge of the structure and content of the English language including the meaning and spelling of words, rules of composition, and grammar.

- *Production and Processing* - Knowledge of raw materials, production processes, quality control, costs, and other techniques for maximizing the effective manufacture and distribution of goods.

Skills:

- *Science* - Using scientific rules and methods to solve problems.

- *Reading Comprehension* - Understanding written sentences and paragraphs in work-related documents.

- *Instructing* - Teaching others how to do something.

- *Active Learning* - Understanding the implications of new information for both current and future problem-solving and decision-making.

- *Learning Strategies* - Selecting and using training/instructional methods and procedures appropriate for the situation when learning or teaching new things.

Abilities:

- *Information Ordering* - The ability to arrange things or actions in a certain order or pattern according to a specific rule or set of rules (e.g., patterns of numbers, letters, words, pictures, mathematical operations).

- *Problem Sensitivity* - The ability to tell when something is wrong or is likely to go wrong. It does not involve solving the problem, only recognizing there is a problem.

- *Deductive Reasoning* - The ability to apply general rules to specific problems to produce answers that make sense.

- *Near Vision* - The ability to see details at close range (within a few feet of the observer).

- *Oral Expression* - The ability to communicate information and ideas in speaking so others will understand.

- *Selective Attention* - The ability to concentrate on a task over a period of time without being distracted.

Available Research Tools

The following is a sample list of available tools to help you in your research:

Tool	Description or URL
Your Steps Toward Success	The Your Steps Toward Success website provides career information as well as links to career tools. www.YourStepsTowardSuccess.com
Career Voyages	The Career Voyages website provides information on the educational opportunities and requirements for occupations. It also contains helpful fact sheets and videos. www.CareerVoyages.org
U.S. Employment Services	The publicly funded workforce system provides One-Stop Career Centers throughout the country. One-Stop Career Centers provide free career counseling to local citizens. www.servicelocator.org
America's Career InfoNet	America's Career InfoNet is a resource for making informed career decisions. www.acinet.org
Occupational Information Network (O*Net)	The Occupational Information Network (O*Net) website provides detailed information about occupations such as the description, tasks, knowledge, skills, abilities, work activities, work context, job zone, apprenticeship opportunities, interests, work values, salary, etc. http://online.onetcenter.org
Career One Stop	Career One Stop is an integrated suite of national websites that help businesses, job seekers, students, and workforce professionals find employment and career resources. www.careeronestop.org
School Career Centers	Most school career centers offer career counseling, on-campus interviews, and job listings. In addition, faculty members may be able to suggest possible career options that have been pursued by previous graduates.
Professional Organizations and/or Industry Associations	Professional organizations and industry associations have web career links, conferences, and career-related activities.

Tool	Description or URL
Online Job Boards	Online job boards not only post available jobs, but they also contain career information.
U.S. Bureau of Labor Statistics	The Bureau of Labor Statistics is the principal fact-finding agency for the U.S. Federal Government in the broad field of labor economics and statistics. It provides detailed information about industry growth and occupational outlooks. www.bls.gov
Bridges	Bridges offers online career tests, career counseling, and job search advice. www.bridges.com

Activity—Researching Interesting Occupations

Purpose

The purpose of this activity is to identify and research the industries and occupations you are interested in learning more about.

Process

- Complete the self-analysis earlier in the lesson on pages 4-6.
- Identify the industries you are interested in.
- Identify the occupations you are interested in.
- Research the growth patterns of the industries you are interested in.
- Research the knowledge, skills, and abilities of the occupations you are interested in.

Research

List the industries you are interested in researching.

_____

_____

_____

List the occupations you are interested in researching.

_____

_____

_____

Industry: _____

Growth Pattern Research:

_____

_____

_____

_____

_____

_____

_____

_____

Industry: _____

Growth Pattern Research:

_____

_____

_____

_____

_____

_____

_____

_____

Industry: _____

Growth Pattern Research:

_____

_____

_____

_____

_____

_____

_____

_____

Occupation: _____

Knowledge, Skills, and Abilities Required:

_____
_____
_____
_____
_____
_____
_____
_____

Occupation: _____

Knowledge, Skills, and Abilities Required:

_____
_____
_____
_____
_____
_____
_____
_____

Occupation: _____

Knowledge, Skills, and Abilities Required:

_____
_____
_____
_____
_____
_____
_____

Training and Education Plan

Each occupation will require some type of training or education. As you research each occupation you are interested in pursuing, develop a training and education plan for that occupation. Identify the available training providers and list the requirements for entry into the training.

Occupation: _____

Training and Certifications Required:

_____

_____

_____

Training Providers:

_____

_____

_____

Requirements to Enter Training:

_____

_____

Occupation: _____

Training and Certifications Required:

_____

_____

_____

Training Providers:

_____

_____

_____

Requirements to Enter Training:

_____

_____

Occupation: _____

Training and Certifications Required:

_____

_____

_____

Training Providers:

_____

_____

_____

Requirements to Enter Training:

_____

_____

Occupation: _____

Training and Certifications Required:

_____

_____

_____

Training Providers:

_____

_____

_____

Requirements to Enter Training:

_____

_____

Informational Interviews

After you have conducted your research, you are ready to interview experts in your desired occupations. Informational interviews can be as casual as having a conversation at an event or can be as formal as visiting an individual at his or her place of employment.

Informational interviews should help you learn more about the realities of the occupation. Questions you could ask during your informational interviews may include:

- What tasks do you perform on a day-to-day basis?

- Can you describe your work environment?

- What companies employ your type of skills?

- What knowledge, skills, and abilities do I need to be employed in your industry?

- Do you enjoy what you do?

- What advice do you have for an individual who would like to pursue your occupation?

In order to have a better understanding about the occupation, you need to ask all of your questions.

If you are going to conduct a formal informational interview, be professional by dressing appropriately and preparing your questions prior to the meeting. (During the Landing the Job You Want module of this career resource workbook, you will learn about interviewing techniques on pages 72-85.)

You should conduct numerous informational interviews in a variety of industries so that you are well-versed in all of your available career options.

List the individuals you could interview.

Individual: *Industry and Occupation:*

_____   _____

_____   _____

_____   _____

_____   _____

_____   _____

Document what you learned from the interviews.

_____

_____

_____

_____

Job Shadowing

Job shadowing is a great opportunity to see first-hand the details of an occupation. Your educational institution may have connections with local businesses for job shadowing opportunities. If not, you should check with your community-based organizations and local One-Stop Career Centers to see if they are aware of any opportunities. Ultimately, you could always ask the individuals you interviewed if their companies allow job shadowing. Many professionals would be flattered that you are interested in learning more about their occupation.

Identify individuals you would like to job shadow.

Individual: *Industry and Occupation:*

_____   _____

_____   _____

_____   _____

_____   _____

_____   _____

Document what you learned from your job shadowing experiences.

_____

_____

_____

_____

_____

_____

_____

_____

_____

_____

_____

_____

_____

Career Videos

Viewing videos about a career is another way to observe first-hand the tasks of an occupation. You can find and view career videos on the Internet. For links to career videos, visit the **www.YourStepsTowardSuccess.com** website.

Employability Skills

Purpose

This lesson will outline the soft skills/employability skills employers are looking for when identifying successful candidates for employment.

Objectives

Check each objective upon completion.

☐ List the soft skills/employability skills employers identified.

☐ Discuss the top ten qualities employers desire in candidates.

☐ Explain the educational foundation employers expect candidates to possess.

Soft Skills/Employability Skills

Employers look for candidates with basic soft skills—these are skills that are not taught on the job. Soft skills are also referred to as employability skills.

Below is a list of soft skills that employers have identified as important for employees to possess:

- Ability to arrive on time to work
- Ability to anticipate problems and develop solutions
- Ability to be productive
- Ability to coach or train others
- Ability to develop strategies
- Ability to multi-task
- Ability to solve problems
- Ability to think analytically
- Ability to think critically
- Attention to detail
- Commitment to ongoing learning
- Flexibility
- Management skills
- Motivation
- Organizational skills
- Project management skills
- Strong interpersonal communication skills, both oral and written
- Strong work ethic
- Team orientation
- Time management skills
- Understanding of basic business principles, such as return on investment and profit/loss
- Understanding of computers
- Understanding of process management
- Values of honesty and integrity

Activity—Obtain the Qualities Desired by Employers

Purpose

The purpose of this activity is to provide you the opportunity to develop the qualities employers desire in employees.

Process

- Identify a quality desired by employers that you do not possess.
- Identify how you are going to develop the quality.
- Actively develop the quality.
- Report on how you developed the quality.

For Example:

Quality: *Arrive on time to work*

Activities to help me develop the quality:
Think through the details of what needs to happen for me to arrive on time. For example, how much time do I need to get ready? How long is my commute with traffic? To be on time, I should leave 15 minutes earlier than needed in case of unforeseen circumstances.

Try to arrive on time to school and any other planned activity.

Documentation on the way I developed the quality:
Every time I had an appointment or had to be somewhere at a certain time, I calculated when I needed to leave to be on time. For example, if I had to be somewhere at 8:00 a.m. and it took me 30 minutes to get ready, 20 minutes to drive to my destination, and 15 minutes for errors, then I got up at 6:55 a.m. and left my house by 7:25 a.m.

*Quality:*_____

Activities to help me develop the quality:

_____
_____
_____
_____
_____

Documentation on the way I developed the quality:

_____
_____
_____
_____
_____
_____

*Quality:*_____

Activities to help me develop the quality:

_____
_____
_____
_____
_____

Documentation on the way I developed the quality:

_____
_____
_____
_____
_____
_____

*Quality:*_____

Activities to help me develop the quality:

_____

_____

_____

_____

_____

Documentation on the way I developed the quality:

_____

_____

_____

_____

_____

_____

_____

*Quality:*_____

Activities to help me develop the quality:

_____

_____

_____

_____

_____

Documentation on the way I developed the quality:

_____

_____

_____

_____

_____

_____

_____

Top Ten Qualities Employers Seek

The top ten personal qualities/skills employers seek, according to National Association of Colleges and Employers' *Job Outlook 2006* survey, are as follows:

- Communication skills (verbal and written)
- Honesty/integrity
- Teamwork skills (works well with others)
- Strong work ethic
- Analytical skills
- Flexibility/adaptability
- Interpersonal skills (relates well to others)
- Motivation/Initiative
- Computer skills
- Detail-oriented

Activity—Define the Top Ten Qualities

Purpose

Since the qualities above are important for applicants to possess, the purpose of this activity is to help you understand each quality and identify activities to help you develop each quality.

Process

- Define and analyze each quality.
- Determine if you currently possess the quality.
- If you do not currently possess the quality, then identify activities that will help you develop the quality.
- If you feel like you already possess the quality, then identify activities that will help you strengthen or improve the quality.

For Example:

Communication skills (verbal and written)

Definition: *The exchange of thoughts, messages, or information, using speech, signals, writing or behavior. The art and technique of using words effectively to convey information or ideas.*

Do I possess the quality? *No / Yes*

If not, how do I obtain it? *Practice communicating my thoughts to individuals who can provide me feedback on ways I can improve my communication skills.*

If yes, how can I improve? *Apply effective communication techniques, such as active listening.*

Communication skills (verbal and written)

Definition: _____

_____

_____

Do I possess the quality? _____

If not, how do I obtain it? If yes, how can I improve? _____

_____

Honesty/Integrity

Definition: _____

_____

_____

Do I possess the quality? _____

If not, how do I obtain it? If yes, how can I improve? _____

_____

Teamwork Skills

Definition: _____

_____

_____

Do I possess the quality? _____

If not, how do I obtain it? If yes, how can I improve? _____

_____

Strong Work Ethic

Definition:

_____

_____

_____

Do I possess the quality?
_____

If not, how do I obtain it? If yes, how can I improve?

_____

Analytical Skills

Definition:

_____

_____

_____

Do I possess the quality?
_____

If not, how do I obtain it? If yes, how can I improve?

_____

Flexibility and Adaptability

Definition:

_____

_____

_____

Do I possess the quality?
_____

If not, how do I obtain it? If yes, how can I improve?

_____

Interpersonal Skills

Definition:

_____

_____

_____

Do I possess the quality?
_____

If not, how do I obtain it? If yes, how can I improve?

_____

Motivation and Initiative

Definition: _____

_____

_____

Do I possess the quality? _____

If not, how do I obtain it? If yes, how can I improve? _____

_____

Computer Skills

Definition: _____

_____

_____

Do I possess the quality? _____

If not, how do I obtain it? If yes, how can I improve? _____

_____

Detail-oriented

Definition: _____

_____

_____

Do I possess the quality? _____

If not, how do I obtain it? If yes, how can I improve? _____

_____

Note: The quality definitions are located on page 169.

Along with soft skills, employers also expect that candidates will have a strong academic foundation in basic math, science, reading, and computers. This foundation can be gained through formal education, apprenticeship, or other training methods, such as internships.

As a potential employee, you do not have to possess all of the skills the employers identified; however, employers will try and find candidates to fill the gaps that exist in their companies. Employers need to have a competitive workforce that possesses an effective combination of the attributes and characteristics identified in this lesson.

SUCCESS Through Goal Setting

Purpose

The purpose of setting goals is to achieve success. This lesson will teach you how to achieve SUCCESS through goal setting.

Objectives

Check each objective upon completion.

☐ Discuss the importance of goal setting.

☐ Explain how to achieve SUCCESS through goal setting.

☐ Set two professional goals.

Goal Setting

Goals keep individuals and organizations focused on achieving a vision. When individuals and organizations set goals, they are taking the first step toward success. Goal setting allows individuals and organizations to determine both their priorities and the actions needed to achieve their goals.

What is your experience with goal setting?

_____

_____

_____

_____

_____

_____

_____

_____

Why is it important to set goals?

_____

_____

_____

_____

_____

_____

_____

_____

_____

_____

_____

_____

_____

Successful Goal Setting

Since effective goals have to meet certain criteria, an easy way to guarantee that you set effective goals is to follow the "S.U.C.C.E.S.S." goal setting steps. The SUCCESS goal setting steps can be used to set your own personal and professional goals.

The following table describes SUCCESS through goal setting:

S.U.C.C.E.S.S.	Description	Questions to Ask
Start	You must be specific about what you want to accomplish. You must write down what you will do and how you are going to accomplish the goal.	• What do I want to accomplish? • What steps do I need to take to accomplish this goal? • What resources do I need to accomplish this goal? • What is my deadline?
Understand	To achieve the goal, you must understand the details of the goal.	• Whom do I need to work with to achieve this goal? • What do I need to do to achieve this goal? • When do I need to achieve this goal? • Where do I need to be in my career to achieve this goal? • How can I achieve this goal?
Controllable	You must have the control to access the resources necessary to accomplish the goal.	• Do I have the resources to accomplish this goal? • Do I have the capabilities to accomplish this goal? • Do I have the means to accomplish this goal?
Conquerable	The goal must be attainable.	• Is this a short-term or long-term goal? • Is this goal realistic? • How will I know if I have succeeded?

S.U.C.C.E.S.S.	Description	Questions to Ask
Exciting	The goal has to motivate you.	• Does this goal create passion in my heart and soul? • Do I have a burning desire to achieve this goal? • Does this goal excite me?
Stretch	The goal must make you stretch beyond your normal limits.	• Will this goal cause me to stretch and grow? • Will achieving this goal help and provide value to others? • If I achieve this goal, will I be able to give more?
Start Over	Once you have achieved your goal, you need to evaluate your actions and set another goal.	• Did I reach my goal? • What do I want to accomplish now?

For Example:

Goal: Obtain my Bachelor of Science degree with a major in Business within four years.	
Start	*I must identify the courses I need to complete, meet with a career counselor, and register for the classes.*
Understand	*I will have a chart outlining the courses I need to take and when I will take them. I will have a meeting with a career counselor.*
Controllable	*I have the capabilities to accomplish this goal and I will spend three hours this Saturday researching the classes.*
Conquerable	*I have graduated high school and have been accepted to a college. Through this goal, I will be able to gain knowledge and will know that I have succeeded when I receive my diploma.*
Exciting	*Obtaining my B.S. degree will be very exciting. I am excited for the opportunity to achieve this goal.*
Stretch	*When I have my degree, I will be able to teach others and provide guidance and encouragement to those who are trying to obtain a B.S. degree.*
Start Over	*Now that I have obtained my B.S. degree, my next goal will be to secure employment.*

Activity—SUCCESS Through Setting Goals

Purpose

The purpose of this activity is to set two professional goals.

Process

Write two professional goals using the SUCCESS goal setting method.

Goal:	
Start	
Understand	
Controllable	
Conquerable	
Exciting	
Stretch	
Start Over	

Goal:	
Start	
Understand	
Controllable	
Conquerable	
Exciting	
Stretch	
Start Over	

Summary

Once you have completed the following, then you are ready to land the job you want:

- ❑ Conducted a self-analysis

- ❑ Researched occupations in high growth industries

- ❑ Determined occupational demand for the occupations you are interested in pursuing

- ❑ Determined occupational knowledge, skills and abilities for the occupations you are interested in pursuing

- ❑ Developed a training and education plan

- ❑ Conducted informational interviews

- ❑ Took advantage of job shadowing opportunities

- ❑ Obtained the qualities desired by employers

- ❑ Set two professional goals

Landing The Job You Want

Successful Job Searching

Purpose

The purpose of this lesson is to discuss how to successfully search for employment by tapping into the job market.

Objectives

Check each objective upon completion.

❑ Explain the different methods available to search for employment.

❑ Discuss effective job search techniques.

❑ List the online job search resources and useful links.

Job Search Methods

People use a variety of methods to find information about job openings. Some may read the want ads, others ask friends or relatives, and others may contact employers directly. Successful job seekers use a wide variety of job search methods, but they focus most of their time and energy on the most effective job search methods.

Consider the advantages of some of the more common job search methods used by job seekers:

Method	Advantages
Career Fairs	These events offer an important opportunity to gather information and talk with potential employers. Follow up with the employers in whom you have the greatest interest.
School Career Centers	Most school career centers offer career advising, on-campus interviews, and job listings. In addition, faculty members may be able to suggest possible career options that have been pursued by previous graduates. There are some employers that recruit exclusively through schools' career centers, so if you aren't registered with your school's career center you may miss out on some good opportunities.
Professional Organizations	If you belong to a professional organization, take advantage of any programs, web career links, conferences, or other career-related activities offered by the organization. Don't be afraid to share your résumé with people who may be able to assist you.
Corporate Websites	Most companies consider their corporate websites vital components of their recruiting efforts. In order to streamline your communication with a corporation, send your résumé directly to the company through its website.
Online Job Boards	Online job boards allow you to apply electronically for numerous positions. Most online job boards allow you to register for job agents that automatically send you notices of new positions that match your profile. To maximize your job search efforts, sign up for the automatic notices on the job boards that directly relate to your choice of occupation. Some online job boards are America's Job Bank <ajb.org>, Monster.com, and HotJobs.com.

Method	Advantages
Personal Contacts	Most jobs are found through personal contacts. (The "Networking Effectively" lesson on pages 44-48 will teach you how to successfully network.)
Private Employment Services (Head Hunters)	Private employment services can connect you with potential employers. Employers may pay a fee or you as the job seeker may pay a fee for their services.
Targeted Résumé	Contacting an employer and sending your résumé to a specific person will increase your chance of obtaining an interview.
U.S. Employment Services	The publicly funded workforce system provides One-Stop Career Centers throughout the country to assist job seekers with their search for employment. To find your closest One-Stop Career Center, access the www.servicelocator.org website.
Want Ads	Want ads are easily accessed through newspapers and online job boards.

Activity—What Search Methods Are You Going To Use?

Purpose

The purpose of this activity is for you to determine what job search methods would be best for you.

Process

- List the methods you are going to use to search for employment.
- Identify the contact information for each resource (i.e. website URL, address, phone number, etc.).
- Set a goal date for accessing the resource and submitting your résumé.

Method	Contact Information	Goal Date
Example: Online Job Boards: America's Job Bank, Monster, Hot Jobs	America's Job Bank- www.ajb.org Monster – www.monster.com Hot Jobs – www.hotjobs.com	XX/XX/XX

Effective Job Search Techniques

Searching for employment is time-consuming. Use the following job search techniques to effectively search for a job:

Start as soon as possible

- Begin searching for a job as soon as you know you are going to need a job.

- Prepare both a paper résumé and an electronic résumé. (Always keep an updated résumé on a CD, disk, or jump drive.)

Research potential employers

- Visit companies' websites and research their products, services, missions, goals, and open employment opportunities.

Take advantage of any tools

- If a company offers application tools such as a profiling questionnaire, complete it in full and take advantage of the opportunity to showcase your experience.

- If an online job board offers automatic alerts or profiles, sign up for them. For example, Monster.com allows you to sign up for alerts when a job that meets your criteria is posted.

Document your research and applications

- Prepare a tracking sheet that allows you to document the following:

  - Company Name

  - Position Title and Position Description

  - Where you heard about the Job Announcement (URL, friend, etc.)

  - Contact Information for the Company's Human Resource Department

  - Record of Events (date of résumé and cover letter submission, date of follow-ups and to whom you spoke, date of interview, etc.)

  (Download a free electronic template for tracking your applications from the **www.YourStepsTowardSuccess.com** website.)

Be patient and persistent

- Keep at it! A job search takes time and effort and rarely produces results immediately.

Online Job Search Resources and Useful Links

The Internet contains a wealth of information and resources that can assist in every aspect of securing employment. Employers are encouraging applicants to apply for jobs electronically. Individual employer sites, as well as online job boards, can provide you with employment opportunities and other useful career information.

The next few pages will provide you with a list of online job boards and resources. For direct access to the following links, visit the **www.YourStepsTowardSuccess.com** website.

Adguide's College Recruiter Site
www.adguide.com

America's Employers
www.americasemployers.com

America's Job Bank
www.ajb.org

Backdoor Jobs
www.backdoorjobs.com

Better Business Bureau
www.bbb.org

Bureau of Labor Statistics
www.bls.gov

Campus Career Center
www.campuscareercenter.com

Career Builder
www.careerbuilder.com

Career City
www.careercity.com

Career Exchange
www.careerexchange.com

Career Magazine
www.careermag.com

Career Mosaic
www.careermosaic.com

CareerPath
www.careerpath.com

Career Resource Center
www.careers.org

Career Shop
www.careershop.com

Careersite
www.careersite.com

Careers 2000
www.careerconferences.com

Careertech.com
www.careertech.com

CareerWeb
www.careerweb.com

CareerXRoads
www.careerxroads.com

College Central Network - Student Central
www.studentcentral.com

College Grad Job Hunter
www.collegegrad.com

College Recruiter
www.collegerecruiter.com

Get Work Network, Inc.
www.getwork.net

HeadHunter Net
www.HeadHunter.Net

Hoover's Career Opportunity Online
www.hoovers.com

Hot Jobs
www.hotjobs.com

Internet Career Connection
www.iccweb.com

Internet Job Source Magazine
www.statejobs.com

JobBankUSA
www.jobbankusa.com

JobDirect
www.jobdirect.com

Job-Hunt
www.job-hunt.org

Job Options
www.joboptions.com

Job Postings
www.jobpostings.net

Job Profiles
www.jobprofiles.com

JobSourceNetwork
www.jobsourcenetwork.com

JOBTRAK
www.jobtrak.com

Jobweb
www.jobweb.org/search/jobs

+Jobs America
www.plusjobs.org

Monster Board
www.monster.com

My JobSearch
www.myjobsearch.com

Nation Job Network
www.nationjob.com

National Business/Employment Weekly
www.nbew.com

Net-Temps
www.net-temps.com

Network Resource Group
www.nrgjobs.com

Next Wave
www.nextwave.org

Office Team
www.officeteam.com

Princeton Review
www.review.com

RECRUITLogics Inc.
www.recruitlogics.com

Recruiters On-line Network
www.ipa.com

Science Careers
www.sciencecareers.org

Starting Point
www.stpt.com

Student Center
www.StudentCenter.com

Telecommuting Jobs
www.tjobs.com

Tripod
www.tripod.com

Wall Street Journal Career Information
www.careers.wsj.com

U.S. News
www.usnews.com

Wanted Jobs
www.wantedjobs.com

Vault Reports
www.VaultReports.com

Wet Feet
www.wetfeet.com

Networking Effectively

Purpose

The purpose of this lesson is to teach you how to network effectively.

Objectives

Check each objective upon completion.

- ❑ List the categories of potential contacts.

- ❑ Describe the tools for effective networking.

- ❑ Explain how to build your network.

- ❑ Discuss how to network by telephone.

Potential Contacts

The following individuals can be contacted for networking purposes:

- ✓ Friends
- ✓ Neighbors
- ✓ Social Acquaintances
- ✓ Classmates
- ✓ Local Alumni
- ✓ Relatives
- ✓ Politicians
- ✓ Professors

- ✓ Chamber of Commerce Members
- ✓ Church Members
- ✓ Trade Association Members
- ✓ Professional Organization Executives and Members
- ✓ People You've Met at Conferences
- ✓ Speakers You've Met at Conferences

Activity—Whom Are You Going To Contact?

Purpose

The purpose of this activity is to determine who you are going to contact about employment opportunities.

Process

- List the names of the people you are going to contact to discuss employment opportunities.
- Research and record the contact information for each individual.
- Set a goal date for contacting each person.

Name	Contact Information	Goal Date
Example: John Doe	*1-800-123-4567*	*XX/XX/XX*

Tools for Networking

You will need a system for organizing your contacts' names, telephone numbers, email addresses, conversation summaries, follow-up notes, and future networking activities. You must use a system that is comfortable for you. Three-by-five-inch index cards, spiral notebooks, personal organizers, or an electronic database are all options for organizing your contacts.

Your network file should contain the following information on each contact:

- Name of Contact (first and last names)
- Occupation
- Position Title
- Company Name
- Contact Information: Address, Telephone Number, Email Address (business and personal)
- How you Met
- Date of Meeting
- One Outstanding Point about the Person (can serve as a memory trigger)
- Conversation Summary

When you contact the individual, you should note the following items in his or her file:

- Names of individuals he or she recommended you speak with (referrals)
- Dates you followed up on the referrals
- Dates of thank you letters sent to the individuals

(Download a free electronic template for organizing your contacts from the **www.YourStepsTowardSuccess.com** website.)

Building Your Network

It is important to continually build your network. Your network should never stop growing. The following steps will help you build your network:

- **Always exchange contact information with people you meet**

  You never know when you'll need to call a person you met at a conference, a restaurant, or on a plane for job recommendations or leads.

- **Always listen for opportunities**

  Many times you'll hear of job opportunities from your network—you may learn about an employer who is hiring before the job is posted or advertised.

- **Build a network at work**

  Build a reputation at work by becoming knowledgeable in a certain area, sharing credit with others, and/or mentoring new hires. You also want to continually maintain visibility through teaching, writing, speaking, and leading so that your co-workers and superiors notice your work.

- **Always be professional, on the job and in your personal life**

  Always be helpful to and honest with others. The Golden Rule is an important rule to follow. You never know whom you may help or influence or who is watching.

- **Do favors for people**

  If someone asks you to do something for him or her, take advantage of the opportunity. In the future, that individual may be able to do you a favor and introduce you to his or her network.

Telephone Networking Techniques

Networking by telephone can be as effective as meeting with people in person, especially when contacting acquaintances. People live busy lives, but they still want to help. Most people would prefer to help you in ten minutes over the telephone, than meet with you in person for 30 minutes.

Here are ten tips on how you can network for job leads over the telephone:

1. Give a brief introduction: who you are, why you are calling, and what help you need.

2. Ask if this is a good time to talk for ten minutes. If not, ask for a good time to call back. Call back at that time.

3. Ask if he or she may know about job openings pertinent to your career goals.

4. Tell him or her you don't expect an immediate answer. Ask if you can call him or her back at a specific date and time. Usually seven days is a good waiting period; if you wait any longer, your contact may have forgotten you called.

5. Write and send a follow-up email and attach your résumé.

6. Follow up at the time scheduled. Use your networking record to keep track of follow-ups.

7. Be appreciative for whatever information your contacts provide.

8. When a contact gives you names of job leads, ask him or her if he or she will call ahead and make a brief introduction for you before you call. If he or she doesn't agree to do this, ask if you can use his or her name as a referral.

9. Follow up with every lead you are given. It's a good idea to write a 30-second script describing who you are and why you are calling. Always use the name of the individual who referred you as quickly as possible to establish rapport.

10. Keep in touch with your contacts and the individuals they referred. Send them emails to thank them for their time and include your résumé for future reference and distribution. These people can easily become part of your inner network and you want to be a part of their networks.

Writing a Winning Résumé and Cover Letter

Purpose

The purpose of this lesson is to explain how to write a winning résumé and cover letter.

Objectives

Check each objective upon completion.

- ❑ Define the importance of a résumé.

- ❑ Describe how to write an effective résumé.

- ❑ Explain the different types of résumés.

- ❑ Define the importance of a cover letter.

- ❑ Describe how to write an effective cover letter.

- ❑ Describe how to create an electronic application.

Résumé Purpose

A résumé is a tool that advertises your qualifications to prospective employers in an outline form. Your résumé may be your only chance to tell an employer about the skills, experiences, and training that qualify you for the job opening. Your résumé should contain all the facts that show you qualify for the position, and it needs to be customized for each position. The items you choose to highlight should closely match the requirements stated in the job description. It is important for you to take time to write a winning résumé.

Conducting Research

Before you can write a winning résumé, you must conduct some preliminary research. Your research will help you identify the content for your résumé. Put yourself in the position of the employers. Envision what they are looking for in a successful applicant and think about your qualifications and accomplishments. The employers who screen your résumé don't need a job description of your previous positions; they need to know what you have accomplished. Accomplishments provide the content for your résumé and cover letter. Accomplishments allow you to state your talents, skills, knowledge, and strengths, as well as provide concrete evidence that you are as good as you say you are.

During your preliminary research, ask yourself the following questions:

What knowledge, skills, and abilities is the company/employer looking for in prospective employees?

_____

_____

_____

Which of my qualifications are relevant to the job?

_____

_____

_____

What in my background best proves that I can do the job?

_____

_____

_____

Should I put my emphasis on my skills, where I've worked, or on the courses that I've taken in school?

_____

What are my major selling points?

_____

_____

_____

What have I accomplished?

_____

_____

_____

What did I positively change at my previous place of employment or at school?

_____

_____

_____

Have I resolved a long-standing problem?

_____

_____

_____

Have I discovered a new and better approach for getting things done?

_____

_____

_____

Have I saved time, materials, or paperwork?

_____

_____

_____

Have I simplified procedures, processes, or improved services?

_____

_____

_____

Have I taken on any extra responsibilities above and beyond my job description?

_____

_____

_____

What work teams have I led or actively participated in?

_____

_____

_____

What have my supervisors commended me for doing?

_____

_____

_____

The employers who screen your résumé don't need a job description of your previous positions; they need to know what you have accomplished. Accomplishments provide the content for your résumé and cover letter. Accomplishments allow you to state your talents, skills, knowledge, and strengths, as well as provide concrete evidence that you are as good as you say you are.

Formatting Tips

Your résumé must be visually appealing in order to make a good impression on your potential employer.

Apply the following formatting tips to your résumé:

Leave adequate white space	Space without copy, or wording, provides easy and quick readability.
Choose one readable font	Times New Roman is a safe font – use only one.
Use black ink	More than one color does not look professional on a résumé.
Line up major headings	Use the same font characteristics for all headings for easy readability.
Highlight the points you want the reader to notice	Use italics or boldface to highlight the most important information.
Use appropriately-sized bullets	Bullets break up the monotony of the résumé.
Make it visually appealing and easy to read	Use italics, underline, bold, dashes, dots or asterisks to guide the reader's eye.
Use white or cream-colored cardstock or linen paper	The information contained on the résumé, not the color, should catch the employer's eye.
Print your résumé on high-quality paper and use a high-quality printer	A résumé produced on high-quality paper and printed with a high-quality printer signifies a serious applicant.
Limit your résumé to two pages	If necessary, you can use two pages, but a résumé should never be longer than two pages.

Writing Guidelines

Your résumé must be well written in order for the employer to consider your application.

To have an impressive résumé apply the following writing guidelines:

Be concise	Short phrases are easier to read than long sentences and paragraphs.
State accomplishments	Define your accomplishments by using numbers, percentages, or dollar amounts, when possible.
Proofread your résumé	Have at least three other people proofread your résumé to make sure all spelling, grammar, punctuation, and information is correct.
Use action verbs	Action verbs signify accomplishments.

Résumé Rules

Résumés should not contain the following:

- A poor layout or physical appearance
- Misspellings, bad grammar, or incorrect punctuation
- Lengthy phrases, sentences, or paragraphs
- Graphics, drawings, or pictures
- Exaggerations or false information
- Extra marks or copying errors
- Irrelevant information
- Unexplained time gaps between jobs and/or education

Action Verbs

- accelerated
- accomplished
- achieved
- adapted
- administered
- analyzed
- approved
- completed
- conceived
- conducted
- controlled
- coordinated
- created
- delegated
- demonstrated
- directed
- designed
- developed
- earned
- effected
- eliminated
- established
- evaluated
- expanded
- expedited
- facilitated
- found
- generated
- implemented
- improved
- increased
- influenced
- initiated
- inspected
- instructed
- interpreted
- launched
- lectured
- led
- maintained
- managed

- mastered
- motivated
- operated
- ordered
- organized
- originated
- participated
- performed
- pinpointed
- planned
- prepared
- produced
- programmed
- proposed
- proved
- provided
- purchased
- recommended
- reduced
- reinforced
- reorganized
- revamped
- reviewed
- revised
- scheduled
- set up
- simplified
- solved
- streamlined
- structured
- supervised
- supported
- surpassed
- taught
- trained
- translated
- used
- utilized
- won
- wrote

Résumé Content

The following is an example of what should be included in a résumé:

1. NAME, MAILING ADDRESS, TELEPHONE NUMBER, and EMAIL ADDRESS
   You may provide both school and home mailing addresses. Be sure the email address you provide is professional. For example, if your name is Jane Doe, do not use <cutecheerleader@web.net> instead use < janedoe@web.net>.

2. EDUCATION
   List universities, junior colleges, vocational schools, and obtained degrees and/or certificates. List your major and minor fields of study. Grade averages may be included if you received above a 3.5 GPA. Include educational honors or scholarships. Do not list high school information once you have received training beyond high school.

3. EMPLOYMENT
   Begin with your current or most recent employment and include the following information:
   - *Position (Title)*
   - *Company Name*
   - *Dates Work Began and Ended (Month, Year)*
   - *Describe Necessary Duties and Skills*
   - *Explain Accomplishments Using Action Verbs*

4. VOLUNTEER WORK and/or EXTRACURRICULAR ACTIVITIES

5. SKILLS

6. INTERESTS

7. ACTIVITIES SPECIFIC TO YOUR INDUSTRY
   For example, membership in an organization or publications you wrote.

8. REFERENCES
   Write "References Available Upon Request" and take your references with you to the interview.

Résumé Formats

There is no single standard résumé format. It is important to choose a design that highlights your skills and accomplishments.

There are two basic types of résumés: chronological and functional. A chronological résumé highlights your work history by date. A functional résumé highlights your skills. From these two formats, a number of variations can be developed. The most common variations are combination résumés and targeted résumés.

Combination Résumé   Combines a section that highlights skills and a section on work history containing your job titles, places of employment, dates, responsibilities, and accomplishments.

Targeted Résumé   Focuses on those skills and achievements that relate directly to a very specific job.

The tables on the following pages identify the advantages and disadvantages of the different types of résumé formats. Examples of the different résumé formats can be found on the **www.YourStepsTowardSuccess.com** website.

Which format is best for you? Why?

_____

_____

_____

_____

_____

_____

_____

_____

_____

_____

_____

_____

_____

_____

_____

Résumé Format	Advantages	Disadvantages	Best Used By
Chronological	• Emphasizes employment, rather than skill • Widely used format • Logical flow, easy to read • Showcases growth in skills and responsibilities • Shows promotions and impressive titles • Shows company loyalty	• Emphasizes gaps in employment • Highlights frequent job changes • Emphasizes employment instead of skill development • Emphasizes lack of related experience and career changes • Points out demotions	• Individuals with a steady work record • Individuals with experience that relates directly to the position
Functional	• Emphasizes skills rather than employment history • Organizes a variety of experience (paid and unpaid work, other activities) • Disguises gaps in work record or a series of short-term jobs	• Viewed with suspicion by employers due to lack of information about employment history • De-emphasizes job growth and job titles	• Individuals with no previous employment • Individuals with gaps in employment • Individuals with frequent job changes • Individuals who have developed skills from activities other than employment

Notes:

_____

_____

_____

_____

_____

_____

_____

_____

_____

_____

Résumé Format	Advantages	Disadvantages	Best Used By
Combination	• Highlights most relevant skills and accomplishments • De-emphasizes employment history in less-relevant jobs • Combines skills developed in a variety of jobs or other activities • Minimizes drawbacks such as employment gaps and absence of directly related experience	• Confusing if not well-organized • Requires more effort and creativity to prepare	• Individuals who are changing careers or those in transition • Individuals re-entering the job market after some absence • Individuals who have grown in skills and responsibility • Individuals pursuing the same or similar work as they've had in the past
Targeted	• Personalized to company • Shows research • More impressive to employer • Written specifically to employer's needs and job description	• Confusing if not well-organized • Time-consuming to prepare • Should be revised for each employer	• Everyone—because any of the other formats can be made into a targeted résumé

Notes:

_____

_____

_____

_____

_____

_____

_____

_____

_____

_____

_____

_____

_____

_____

Sample Chronological Résumé

John Doe
1234 Alphabet Drive
Albany, New York 12345
123-456-7890
johndoe@yourstepstowardsuccess.com

EDUCATION

<u>Bachelor of Science in Business Management</u>   **May 2004**
New York University – GPA 3.89

WORK EXPERIENCE

<u>Director of Partnership Development</u>   **September 2005 – Present**
ABC Chamber of Commerce: Albany, New York
- Reported directly to the Chief Operating Officer on the organization's partnership development activities
- Developed and conducted promotions to area businesses, educational institutions and workforce intermediaries
- Designed billboard messages and negotiated pricing
- Conducted direct marketing projects to targeted potential partners
- Increased partnerships by 12% within the first year
- Implemented quarterly partnership networking receptions for partners and potential partners
- Organized and taught an educational series to local businesses on how to build partnerships

<u>Manager of Sales</u>   **May 2004 – September 2005**
Number One Products: Buffalo, New York
- Increased sales by 53%
- Reduced costs by 18%
- Facilitated reorganization of the sales department
- Managed 23 sales representatives across the state of New York
- Provided technical training to sales representatives
- Assisted in the marketing of new product lines

<u>Trainer</u>   **August 2000 – June 2003**
Telemarketing Phones: Albany, New York
- Trained 205 new employees
- Assisted in the development of 22 new training programs
- Developed the visual aids for 13 of the new training programs
- Created motivational sayings and strategically placed them around the office

References Available Upon Request

Sample Functional Résumé

Jane Doe
1234 Alphabet Drive
Albany, New York 12345
123-456-7890
johndoe@yourstepstowardsuccess.com

SUMMARY OF QUALIFICATIONS

Has experience in building high-performing teams through a skilled management style with significant experience in performance-oriented leadership and a proven ability to implement and achieve company goals.

SKILLS AND ACCOMPLISHMENTS

Personnel Management
- Managed and supervised over 105 personnel on a daily basis
- Evaluated employees' performance
- Developed employees' skills and talents to achieve company goals
- Motivated employees to become proactive and creative in their jobs
- Decreased turnover and increased morale by 300%

Administration
- Conducted an internal organizational development study
- Provided recommendations for streamlining staff organization and restructuring work flow and work assignments
- Decreased overtime by 20%
- Executed employee promotions
- Identified opportunities for improvement when utilizing office resources
- Assisted in establishing company goals

Fiscal Management
- Managed a $3 million annual budget

WORK EXPERIENCE

Manager of the Department of Human Resources   October 2003 - Present
ABC Corporation: Albany, New York

Human Resource Assistant Director   May 2002 - October 2003
XYZ Corporation: Albany, New York

EDUCATION

Bachelor of Science in Business Management   May 2003
New York University – GPA 3.75

References Available Upon Request

Cover Letter Purpose

A cover letter is often an employer's first impression of you. It should have a positive impact and entice the reader to want to learn more about you. The cover letter introduces your résumé. It should supplement the information in your résumé, not just repeat it.

Writing a Cover Letter

In order to avoid saying too much or not enough in your cover letter, follow these guidelines:

Be concise	A cover letter is an introduction; make it compelling, personable, and brief. It needs to be customized to the job for which you are applying. A cover letter should never be more than one page.
Address it to a specific person	Call the company and ask for the appropriate person (find out the spelling of the individual's name and his or her title in the company) so you can address the cover letter to the correct individual.
If someone referred you to the company, use the individual's name	Always mention the name of the individual who referred you within the first few sentences.
Print your cover letter on high-quality paper and use a high-quality printer	The cover letter should be printed on the same paper and with the same printer as your résumé.
Proofread your cover letter	Company representatives who review cover letters are looking for reasons to eliminate candidates. Typographical errors, misspellings, and bad grammar are indications that you are too careless and they will disregard your application.

The following is an outline of what you should write in your cover letter:

Your Name (First and Last Name)
Your Mailing Address
City, State Zip Code
Your Phone Number
Your Email Address

Date of Letter

Contact Individual's Name (First and Last Names)
Contact Individual's Title
Company Name
Mailing Address
City, State Zip Code

Dear Mr./Mrs./Ms./Dr. (Contact Individual's Last Name):

First Paragraph: State why you are writing, name the position or type of work for which you are applying, and mention how you heard of the opening or organization (placement center, news media, friend, employment service, or website).

Second Paragraph: Explain why you are interested in working for the company and specify your reasons for desiring this type of work. If you have relevant work experience or related education, be sure to point it out, but do not reiterate your résumé.

Third Paragraph: Emphasize your skills or abilities that relate to the job for which you are applying. Be sure to do this in a confident manner and remember that the reader will view your cover letter as an example of your writing skills.

Fourth Paragraph: Refer the reader to your enclosed résumé or application. Write an appropriate closing by thanking the reader for his or her time and consideration. Pave the way for an interview by indicating your interest in working for the company and the actions you will take to initiate an interview date.

Sincerely,

(Your handwritten signature)

Type your name

Enclosure (Anytime you include an additional document, like your résumé, in the envelope of a letter, you need to type "Enclosure" on the bottom of the letter. This informs the individual opening the letter that another document is enclosed.)

Sample Cover Letter

John Doe
1234 Alphabet Drive
Albany, New York 12345
123-456-7890
johndoe@yourstepstowardsuccess.com

January 1, 2020

Jane Adams
Human Resource Manager
ABC Corporation
987 Numbers Lane
Albany, New York 12345

Dear Ms. Adams:

Thank you for the opportunity to provide ABC Corporation with information about my qualifications for the Account Manager sales position within your organization. I became aware of this job opening from a current ABC Corporation employee by the name of John Smith.

I know that ABC Corporation has the technology, products, and people that are considered top-notch. As part of my career goals, I want to be associated with productive people and a profitable company, like ABC Corporation.

While I studied Technical Sales in college, I managed a sales team for ZYX Corporation. Due to my sales knowledge and leadership skills, my team generated more than $2 million in profits last year. Since graduation, I have been promoted to Senior Sales Manager. Through my sales and marketing efforts, I have been able to establish ZYX Corporation as a differentiator rather than a low-cost alternative. In my current position, I have helped the marketing team market the products through affiliates and by co-branding with other businesses. Our sales conversion rate is extremely high because of my ability to link our products' features directly to how they will benefit the potential client's needs.

I have the desire and the skills that it will take to become a successful long-term asset to ABC Corporation as an Account Manager. Thank you for your time and consideration. I look forward to hearing from you and setting up an interview.

Sincerely,

John Doe

John Doe

Enclosure

Electronic Application

When done properly, the submission of electronic résumés and cover letters can be an efficient use of the Internet when applying for jobs. As with other aspects of performing an electronic job search, you need to become familiar with the requirements of electronic applications prior to submitting your resume and cover letter online.

Important: Prior to submitting your application, you should always read the employer's submission instructions.

What is an Electronic Application?

An electronic application is a résumé and cover letter that is transmitted online to a prospective employer and received directly into the prospective employer's computer system.

Composing an Electronic Application

In order for an electronic application to be received, it must be saved in plain text. This will change the layout and style of your résumé and cover letter, since plain text does not accommodate the same graphic features used in word processing programs. A common application for plain text is Notepad in Windows XP.

Note: The same process can be used for both the résumé and the cover letter.

To prepare a résumé for electronic distribution follow the guidelines below:

1. Compose a résumé using a standard word processing software tool such as Microsoft Word
2. Save the files
3. Open Notepad
4. Copy your résumé from the word processing software
5. Paste your résumé into Notepad
6. Edit the layout of the plain text (Notepad) version of your résumé
7. Copy your résumé from the plain text (Notepad) application
8. Paste your résumé into the body of your email
9. As a test, email the résumé to yourself to see how it looks after being emailed
10. Edit your résumé so that it looks good
11. Send your résumé to potential employers as a plain text document

Sending an Electronic Application

The most common method of transmitting a résumé and cover letter is via email. It is important that your cover letter and résumé are received as one document. There are a few ways this can be done:

1. A cover letter can be composed as the email message, and the résumé, in plain text or a PDF document, can be sent as an attachment to the email.

2. The cover letter and résumé can be imported into the email message by using your software's cut and paste feature.

Résumés and cover letters can also be submitted online through job banks or through a company's website. Since electronic résumés are scanned for important key words, it is important your résumé contains enough information and keywords for the system to select your résumé for consideration. If appropriate, use the same words the employer used in the job description.

Résumé Scanning

Whether sent by mail, fax, or electronically, many résumés today are being scanned to determine an applicant's qualifications or fit for the job. The scanner picks up on keywords that the employer selected. The more keyword matches in your résumé, the greater the likelihood that you will be identified as a strong candidate.

Use the following guidelines when writing a résumé that will be scanned:

*   Your name should be the first item on a résumé, since scanners file résumés under the first line of information.

*   Scanned résumés can be longer than one page because they need to contain enough keywords to qualify you for consideration.

Activity—Creating a Winning Cover Letter and Résumé

Purpose

The purpose of this activity is to create a general cover letter and résumé.

Process

*   Conduct the preliminary research on pages 50-52 to help you identify the content for your résumé.

*   Identify the appropriate résumé format for your experience.

*   Write and format a general résumé and cover letter.

*   Create an electronic cover letter and résumé.

*   Save your general résumé and cover letter on a CD, disk, or jump drive so you can customize each document prior to submitting the documents for employer review.

Developing a Career Portfolio

Purpose

The purpose of this lesson is to develop a career portfolio, which is an essential tool for managing your career.

Objectives

Check each objective upon completion.

- ❑ Describe a career portfolio.

- ❑ Explain the importance of a career portfolio.

- ❑ Describe how to build and maintain a career portfolio.

- ❑ Explain how to use a career portfolio in an interview.

What is a Career Portfolio?

A career portfolio is a tool that will help you organize your accomplishments, skills, work experience, educational background, and awards.

Why Should You Keep a Career Portfolio?

Employers are very results-driven. When they evaluate candidates, they are asking themselves what a candidate can contribute to the success of their company. Utilizing a career portfolio during a job interview will set you apart from other candidates. Like an artist keeps a portfolio of his or her work, your career portfolio is your opportunity to showcase your talents and accomplishments. It is also a strategic way to organize your job search.

Have you ever needed contact information for your references and had to search frantically to find previous supervisors' names, phone numbers, and mailing and email addresses, and phone numbers? A portfolio will solve that problem because it serves as an accurate record of your job history, accomplishments, and background.

How Should You Start to Build Your Portfolio?

The best way to start to build a portfolio is to first give some thought to the knowledge, skills, and abilities you want to emphasize in your portfolio. Consider work products you have produced that illustrate your knowledge, skills, and abilities. The most beneficial way to maintain your portfolio is to compile materials as you complete projects and earn recognition.

What Does a Career Portfolio Contain?

A career portfolio should contain three sections, with each section having its own binder.

The three sections may be divided as follows:

- a section to show employers in job interviews

- a section for your own personal career journal

- a section for your job search record

The next few pages provide suggestions for what to include in these three sections.

Section One: Information for Prospective Employers

This section should be organized with tabs and a table of contents since you will be sharing it with prospective employers. There are a number of ways you can arrange the documents, such as chronologically, by project, by type of experience, or any way you choose. The most important detail is to just be consistent. Some documents to include in this section are:

- Awards and scholarships you received.

- Budgets, financial statements, or annual reports you produced.

- Current résumé.

- Examples of work you've contributed to or completed.

- Information from training sessions, conferences, meetings you attended, such as the date, location, whom you met or heard speak, and what you learned.

- Letters of recommendation.

- Performance evaluations.

- Presentations (i.e., PowerPoint) you designed and/or delivered.

- References with contact information.

- School transcripts.

- Writing samples, such as articles, flyers, manuals, or handbooks.

Section Two: Career Journal – Your Work in Progress

This section is for your own personal use and should not be shared with potential employers. It is your career journal that you should continually update. You should include the following:

- A list of job-related goals, both long-term and short-term, and an outline of intermediate steps to accomplish your goals.

- Copies of your current and past job descriptions and duties you performed.

- History of employers' and managers' contact information.

- Logs of your noteworthy accomplishments that will help you develop Section One of your portfolio for prospective employers.

- Names of organizations you'd like to join, information on conferences you would like to attend, and ideas to further your own professional development.

- Notes from on-the-job and off-the-job networking you've done.

Section Three: Job Search Records

This section helps you organize your job search records. Even if you are not currently job-hunting, it is beneficial to maintain this section, just in case you hear about a job for which you would like to apply.

- A calendar to serve as a timeline for your job search action plan.

- A draft cover letter that you can tailor to apply for a specific job.

- A draft résumé that you can tailor to apply for a specific job.

- Copies of other job search-related correspondence you have sent, such as thank you letters following interviews.

- Job descriptions for jobs that you've applied for, or plan to apply for, and a dated copy of your submitted application.

- Job search articles or names of books and websites you've found helpful that might come in handy when trying to prepare for your interview.

- Notes on upcoming interviews/meetings (include information such as the date, time, with whom you'll be meeting, etc. and information about the company).

- Your job search to do list.

Important Note: Be sure to save your portfolio to a CD, disk, or jump drive for future use.

Using Your Career Portfolio in an Interview

Taking Section One of your career portfolio with you to an interview will leave a positive impression on the prospective employer and make you stand out as a unique candidate.

During the interview, the interviewer may be impressed with your career portfolio and he or she may ask to keep the portfolio for a few days to review your work. This is a good sign so be prepared to leave the portfolio with the interviewer. To be prepared to leave the portfolio use copies of documents rather than originals. Also be sure to review your portfolio so only material relevant to the particular job is included and that the portfolio is well-organized and visually appealing. The more exposure you receive the better chances you have of being hired.

Activity—Creating Your Career Portfolio

Purpose

The purpose of this activity is to create your career portfolio.

Process

- Identify the knowledge, skills, and abilities you want to emphasize in your portfolio.

- Identify and gather work products you have produced.

- Gather available documents (i.e. résumé, references, awards and scholarships, performance evaluations, transcripts, letters of recommendations, etc.)

- Develop a career journal.

- Develop a format for documenting your job search.

- Organize the portfolio into three different sections and binders.

- Scan the files and save them onto a CD, disk, or jump drive.

- Share your portfolio with a friend or family member.

Interview Strategies

Purpose

The purpose of this lesson is to teach you successful interview strategies.

Objectives

Check each objective upon completion.

- ❑ Explain how to prepare for an interview.

- ❑ Describe how to dress for an interview.

- ❑ Discuss the most common interview questions.

- ❑ Discuss the questions you may ask during an interview.

- ❑ List the items on the Pre-Interview Checklist.

- ❑ Describe the guidelines for a successful interview.

- ❑ Explain the purpose of a thank you letter and how to write a thank you letter.

Preparing for the Job Interview

It is important that you prepare for the job interview by doing the following:

- **Research the Company and the Position**

    If you research the company, the interviewer will be impressed by your interest and motivation because most applicants do not do their research. Your knowledge about the company will set you apart from all of the other applicants because you will be able to explain what you can do for the company. You need to know key information about the company, its products and its customers, prior to the interview. In addition, try and find out about the job functions of the position. You can research the company and the position online but if you can talk to people who work for the company or others who may be familiar with the company, then you will gain additional insight into the company's goals and purpose. You should also call the office receptionist so you will know who is interviewing you and how to spell and pronounce his or her name.

- **Practice your answers to the most commonly asked interview questions.**

    During an interview, you will be asked a variety of questions. Your answers to these questions provide the interviewer an insight into your personality, experience, and work habits. It is important that you answer all questions honestly and accurately. You want to appear impressive, so it is critical that you practice your answers to the most commonly asked interview questions prior to the interview. You should practice by having a friend or family member conduct a mock interview with you by asking you the questions on the following pages. To check your diction, speed, and body language, you might want to video tape the mock interview.

- **Prepare a list of questions to ask the employer.**

    Prior to your interview, you should prepare a list of questions to ask the interviewer. It is appropriate to refer to your list of questions during the interview. This shows the interviewer that you took the time to think about what you would like to know about the position or the company. Just as an interview is an opportunity for the company to get to know you, it is also an opportunity for you to get to know the company. The job needs to be a good fit for both parties.

- **Prepare a list of three to five references.**

    References should be previous employers, professors, religious advisors, organization advisors, or friends that are well respected in the business or political arena. Do NOT use family members.

- **Prepare your interview materials the night before the interview.**

- **Take several copies of your résumé, a list of references, a nice pen, and Section One of your career portfolio to the interview.**

Common Interview Questions

During your interview, you do not want to answer the questions asked by the interviewer with a simple "yes" or "no." Therefore, you will want to explain your thoughts whenever possible. You can organize your thoughts by writing your answers to the following interview questions.

Note: For suggestions and examples on how to answer the interview questions, visit the **www.YourStepsTowardSuccess.com** website.

Your Qualifications

Why do you want to work for our organization?

_____

_____

_____

What qualifications do you have that relate to the position?

_____

_____

_____

What can you do for us that someone else can't do?

_____

_____

_____

What new skills or capabilities have you developed recently?

_____

_____

_____

Give me an example, from a previous job, where you've shown initiative.

_____

_____

_____

What have you recently accomplished?

_____

_____

_____

What is important to you in a job?

_____

_____

_____

What motivates you in your work?

_____

_____

_____

What have you been doing since your last job?

_____

_____

_____

What qualities do you find important in a co-worker?

_____

_____

_____

Why should I hire you?

_____

_____

_____

What are your strengths?

_____

_____

_____

What are your weaknesses?

_____

_____

_____

What do you know about our organization?

_____

_____

_____

Do you prefer working with others or by yourself? Why?

_____

_____

_____

What can you tell me about yourself?

_____

_____

_____

Your Career Goals

What are your career goals?

_____

_____

_____

What type of employment position are you interested in?

_____

_____

_____

How does this job fit into your career goals?

_____

_____

_____

What would you like to be doing five years from now?

_____
_____
_____

How do you define success?

_____
_____
_____

How will you achieve success?

_____
_____
_____

What do you expect from this job?

_____
_____
_____

What do you expect to gain from this position?

_____
_____
_____

Are you comfortable with traveling?

_____
_____
_____

When can you start?

_____
_____
_____

Are you willing to relocate?

_____

_____

_____

Your Work Experience

What have you learned from your past jobs?

_____

_____

_____

What responsibilities have you had that were important?

_____

_____

_____

What specific skills from previous jobs will you use for this position?

_____

_____

_____

How does your previous experience relate to this position?

_____

_____

_____

What did you like most/least about your last job?

_____

_____

_____

Whom may we contact for references?

_____

_____

_____

What extracurricular activities have you participated in? What did you learn from them?

_____

_____

_____

Your Education

How do you think your education has prepared you for this position?

_____

_____

_____

What were your favorite classes/activities in school?

_____

_____

_____

Why did you choose to study what you did in school?

_____

_____

_____

Do you plan to continue your education?

_____

_____

_____

Questions for You to Ask

Once the interviewer has asked his or her questions, then he or she might say, "Do you have any questions for me?" It is critical that you take this opportunity to ask questions because asking questions shows that you are sincerely interested in the position and the company.

Some questions you could ask the interviewer include:

- Can you please tell me how your career has developed at XYZ Corporation? Would someone entering the firm today have similar opportunities?

- If I work hard and prove my value to the firm, where might I be in five years?

- What are the opportunities for advancement?

- What goals has your company set?

- What does a typical day look like for the individual in this position?

- How does this position and department contribute to the overall company mission and philosophy?

- What characteristics best describe individuals who are successful in this position?

- Does this position offer exposure to other facets of your organization?

- What other positions and/or departments does this position interact with most?

- To whom does this position report?

- How much decision-making authority and autonomy are given to new employees?

- How will my performance be evaluated?

- How often are performance reviews given? By whom?

- Does your organization encourage its employees to pursue additional education?

- How would you describe the organization's culture/environment?

- What makes your organization different from its competitors?

- What industry-wide trends are likely to affect your organization's strengths and weaknesses?

- How would you describe your organization's personality and management style?

- How is the work environment affected by the organization's management style?

Activity—Mock Interviews

Purpose

The purpose of this activity is to allow you the opportunity to practice interviewing in a safe environment.

Process

- Review your answers to the questions on pages 74-79.

- Ask someone you trust to conduct a mock interview with you by asking you five or more of the questions listed on pages 74-79.

- You, as the interviewee, will then ask the interviewer three questions about the job or the corporation from page 80.

- After you have finished asking your questions, end the interview and ask the mock interviewer to provide you with feedback on your interviewing skills.

Appropriate Interview Dress

You must dress professionally and conservatively for your interview because you will be judged by what you wear.

Women

- A straightforward business suit is best (dark blue or black skirt suit)
- Skirt should be to the knee or below
- Simple blouse (white, cream, or light blue)
- Wear sensible dress shoes
- Wear nylons or stockings
- Make sure bag and shoes are polished
- Be moderate with make-up and perfume
- Wear simple jewelry
- Hair and fingernails should be well-groomed

Men

- A clean, well-pressed white or light blue shirt
- A red, yellow, navy or royal blue tie with a conservative pattern
- Dark blue or black suit
- Shoes must be polished
- Face should be clean-shaven or facial hair should be neatly trimmed
- Hair and fingernails should be well-groomed
- Use cologne or after-shave sparingly

Pre-Interview Checklist

Before leaving for an interview, ask yourself the following questions:

✓ **Attitude** — Am I thinking positively and like a winner?

✓ **Body Scent** — Do I smell good?

✓ **Breath** — Is my breath smelling fresh?

✓ **Career Portfolio** — Is Section One of my career portfolio neat and complete?

✓ **Hair** — Is my hair clean and combed?

✓ **Hands** — Are my hands and nails clean?

✓ **Answers** — Have I practiced my answers to the common interview questions?

✓ **Nice Black Pen** — Do I have a nice black pen with me?

✓ **Attire** — Am I dressed appropriately? Are my clothes pressed and clean?

✓ **Prepared** — Do I have a comb, lint collector, and mints?

✓ **Résumé** — Do I have several neat copies of my résumé in a leather binder?

✓ **References** — Do I have several neat copies of my references?

✓ **Time** — What time do I need to leave to be 15 minutes early?

Guidelines for a Successful Interview

For a successful interview, follow these guidelines:

Arrive early	Arrive at least 15 minutes early. Interviewers interpret being early as evidence of your commitment, dependability, and professionalism.
Introduce yourself in a courteous manner	Give a sincere smile and show openness by leaning into the greeting while shaking hands and making eye contact.
Firm handshake	A firm handshake demonstrates your confidence and professionalism.
Have confidence	Show self-confidence by making eye contact with the interviewer and answering his or her questions in a clear voice.
Use body language to show interest	An interviewer wants to see how well you react under pressure—avoid negative body language, such as looking down.
Be positive and try to make others feel comfortable	Relax; think of the interview as a conversation, not as an interrogation. Remember, the interviewer is also nervous about making a good impression on you.
Listen	Communication should be two-way. If you are talking too much, you will probably miss cues concerning what the interviewer feels is important. On the other hand, if you never talk, the interviewer will think you are disinterested in the conversation.
Reflect before answering a difficult question	If you are unsure how to answer a question, you might reply with another question. For example, if the interviewer asks you what salary you expect, try answering by saying the following: "That is a good question. What are you planning to pay your best candidate?"

Answer inappropriate questions appropriately	In the U.S., illegal interview questions are those that discriminate against you on the basis of age, color, disability, gender, national origin, race, or religion.
	If you are asked an illegal question, tactfully answer the question indirectly.
	When asked about your personal life, you might respond with, "I prefer to keep personal and business matters separate."
	When asked about children, your reply might be, "My personal life will not affect my professionalism."
	When asked about a disability, you might say something like, "I assure you that I will be able to perform the duties of the job."
	When asked about your country of origin, you could say, "I am authorized to work in the United States."
Ask questions you prepared in advance	When it is your turn, ask the questions you have prepared in advance. These should cover any information about the company and job position you could not find in your own research.
	Important: Do not ask questions that raise red flags. Red flag questions would include:
	"Is relocation a requirement?"
	"How many vacation and sick days would I receive?"
Thank the interviewer and ask about the next step in the process	At the end of the interview you could say: "I would really like to work for your organization. I think it is a great opportunity and I am confident I can contribute to its success. What is the next step of the selection process?"
	End the interview with a handshake and thank the interviewer for his or her time. Reiterate your interest in the position and your qualifications. Ask if you can telephone in a few days to check on the status of your application. If they offer to contact you, politely ask when you should expect the call.
Write a thank you letter to anyone you have spoken to	Covered next in this lesson on pages 86-88.

Thank You Letters

A follow-up thank you letter to the interviewer is an important step in the interviewing process. Immediately following the interview, send a thank you letter in an email to the interviewer. Restate your strong points and personalize the note with information you discussed during the interview. A standard thank you letter, sent in the mail, should immediately follow a formal job interview. It is important to send the thank you letter as an email and a formal letter.

Keep the letter short, reiterate major points of the conversation, and express your interest in the position.

Use the following guidelines to help you write an appropriate thank you letter:

- Type the letter using a business letter format. Address the letter to the person with whom you interviewed. Include the interviewer's name, title, organization, and complete mailing address.

- Mention the position for which you interviewed and express your interest in the position and the company.

- Express appreciation for the opportunity to interview, tour the facilities, meet other employees, etc.

- Re-emphasize your most important skills and qualifications and how you expect to contribute to the organization.

- Include any information you forgot to mention in the interview, if necessary (be brief).

- Close your letter with a comment about future contact with the employer.

The following is an outline of what you should write in your thank you letter:

Your Name (First and Last Name)
Your Mailing Address
City, State Zip Code
Your Phone Number
Your Email Address

Date of the Letter

Interviewer's Name (First and Last Names)
Interviewer's Title
Company
Mailing Address
City, State Zip Code

Dear Mr./Ms./Mrs./Dr. (Interviewer's Last Name):

First Paragraph: Thank the interviewer for interviewing you for the position. Make a positive statement about the company and how you would be honored to be a member of its team.

Second Paragraph: Mention two or three items discussed during the interview.

Third Paragraph: Express your interest again and how you will be an asset to the corporation.

Fourth Paragraph: State that you look forward to hearing from him or her regarding a final decision.

Sincerely,

(Your handwritten signature)

Type your name

Sample Thank You Letter

John Doe
1234 Alphabet Drive
Albany, New York 12345
123-456-7890
johndoe@yourstepstowardsuccess.com

February 1, 2020

Jane Adams
Senior Account Manger
ABC Corporation
987 Numbers Lane
Albany, New York 12345

Dear Ms. Adams:

Thank you for the opportunity to discuss the Sales Account Manager position. It was a pleasure meeting you today. I also enjoyed learning more about the position, the product, and the company's goals and values. I am very impressed with the direction the company is going and I have a strong desire to be a part of ABC Corporation's future. As I reflected upon the interview, I feel I will be able to contribute to the success of the company by increasing sales and maximizing customer satisfaction.

During our discussion, I mentioned how I work with a variety of individuals through my current job. One of my strengths is my ability to communicate technical information to individuals who do not have the technical knowledge that I possess. I also know how to treat people with the utmost respect and make sure they know that I value their business. I have no doubt that I have the skills and motivation to be a successful part of the ABC Corporation's Sales Account Management Team.

Through our conversation, I can tell that you truly care about the company, its products, and its clients. I would be proud to be associated with ABC Corporation.

The possibility of working at ABC Corporation makes me very excited. I feel that I am a prime candidate for the Sales Account Manager position because of my strong work ethic, sales knowledge and experience, technical background, and core customer service values.

Thank you again for the opportunity I had to visit with you today. I truly appreciate your time and I look forward to hearing from you.

Sincerely,

John Doe

John Doe

Activity—Creating a Thank You Letter

Purpose

The purpose of this activity is for you to create a thank you letter.

Process

- Write a general thank you letter.

- Format the thank you letter.

- Save your general thank you letter on a CD, disk, or jump drive so you can customize it after each interview.

Negotiating Salary and Benefits

Purpose

The purpose of this lesson is to teach you how to negotiate your salary and benefits so you can create a win-win situation by the end of the negotiation process.

Objectives

Check each objective upon completion.

❑ Explain the negotiation process.

❑ Discuss the guidelines for salary negotiations.

❑ Describe the benefits offered by most companies.

The Negotiation Process

It is important that you follow the process of negotiation in order to achieve your ultimate goal—a win-win conclusion.

Process Step	Description
Preparation	• Research, explore, and consider all the options (your salary requirements and benefits and the employer's expected salary requirements) before entering negotiations. • Identify the available options if a win-win conclusion cannot be reached. What is the lowest salary you are willing to accept? What benefits can compensate for a lower salary? What is the average salary for someone doing a similar job in your geographic location? • Attempt to understand how you can meet both your needs and the employer's needs.
Discussion	• The actual negotiation between you and the employer begins. • There are three phases (Opening, Body, and Closing) of the negotiation process that take place during the discussion step.
Post Negotiation Review	• Evaluate the negotiation process and how you can improve for the next negotiation opportunity.

Phases of the Discussion Step

The three discussion step phases are as follows:

Opening: The opening phase focuses on people and attempts to establish rapport with the individuals involved in the negotiations.

Body: The body phase focuses on discovering and focusing on the interests of the individuals involved in the negotiations.

Closing: The closing phase focuses on inventing options and establishing a mutual agreement between the individuals involved in the negotiations.

Opening: Build Rapport

During the opening phase, the employer attempts to build a relationship with you. The employer will first compliment you on your qualifications and then he or she will let you know the company is interested in making you an offer to join their team.

Body: Discover and Focus on the Interests of the Employer

During the body phase, you and the employer will focus on the compensation package and other employment details, such as your salary requirements and start date.

To be a good negotiator, you need to uncover and focus on the interests of the employer. The employer is interested in hiring you because you have the skills to fill a gap in the company. The employer is also interested in staying within his or her salary budget for the position. The employer may also have other interests in mind, such as filling the position in order to increase profits or filling the position in order to complete a project on time. You need to find out the employer's interests before you begin negotiating your compensation package.

The goal of the body phase is to create a win-win situation with the employer by understanding the employer's interests.

Closing: Invent Options

During the closing phase, you can move toward offering potential options to satisfy the employer's interests. Offering options is a natural step after uncovering the interests of the employer. Often, brainstorming techniques are helpful in inventing options. Once you have focused on business issues, uncovered interests, applied fair standards, and invented options then there is a greater chance that you will be able to reach a win-win conclusion with the employer by the end of the closing phase.

Salary Negotiating Guidelines

Since you don't know when salary negotiations will take place, prepare for the negotiations before you go into the first interview. Most employers won't discuss compensation until they have decided to hire you, but that could be after your first interview.

Use the following guidelines to conduct successful salary negotiations:

- **Research what you are worth**

  It is important for you to know what your skills are worth because it provides you with a foundation for evaluating the offer and negotiating your compensation package. You can begin researching your salary by using resources such as <www.salary.com>, your school career center, professional journals, or the U.S. Bureau of Labor Statistics <www.bls.gov>. You must determine what salary you are willing to take, what compensation is fair, and what you want. Keep in mind, that if you are considering a position in another location, the cost of living may be different and the offer may reflect that difference. Everything is negotiable, from your salary to the number of vacation days you receive.

- **Know when to discuss salary**

  Do not discuss salary until an offer has been extended.

- **Understand how to discuss salary**

  If an employer asks for your salary requirements, he or she is trying to identify a starting point for negotiations. Try to avoid stating a salary requirement. Always state that your salary is negotiable, because the first person to state a price range sets the precedent for the discussion. Wait until the employer states his or her salary range and then extend the range approximately 10 percent. Aim for your desired salary, but be prepared to accept less. If the salary is not acceptable, try and negotiate other types of compensation such as extra vacation days, flex time, or telecommuting options. Never say "yes" to an offer right away; silence can be financially beneficial.

- **Practice what you might say once the employer has stated a price**

    Be realistic, firm, and assertive but not confrontational. State that you are very interested in working for the employer and that you want to work out a win-win compensation package. You may want to consider using the following sample language:

    o "As long as you pay a fair market value and the responsibilities fit my level of skill, I think we can work out a reasonable arrangement. You must have some range in mind. I'll tell you if it's near my competitive value."

    o "Thanks for the offer. I am very excited about working for you because ABC Corporation is my first choice for employment. However, since I have researched the going rate for my skills and knowledge, I was really looking for a salary in the range of $XX,XXX to $XX,XXX. Does your budget allow for a salary within that range?"

- **Get the offer in writing**

    Once you have verbally agreed on your compensation package, make sure the employer sends the offer, including the details of what benefits you negotiated, to you in writing. This binds the employer to his or her verbal commitments.

Benefits Count

Benefits are sometimes included in your compensation package and they cost the corporation an additional 30 – 40% on top of your salary. Prior to any negotiation discussion, you need to determine what benefits you need and what benefits you want. Keep in mind that your offer may or may not include all of the benefits listed on the next page.

Activity—What Benefits Do You Need?

Purpose

The purpose of this activity is to allow you time to determine the benefits you need versus the benefits you want.

Process

- Using the table on the next page, review the benefits.

- Add any additional benefits you need or want that are not listed in the table on the next page.

- Mark each benefit either as a Need or a Want.

- After you have marked the benefits as a Need or a Want, then prioritize the benefits in the left column.

- Evaluate your priorities.

List of Benefits

Priority	Benefit	Need	Want
_____	Child Care Assistance	_____	_____
_____	Dental Insurance	_____	_____
_____	End of Year Bonus	_____	_____
_____	Flexible Spending Accounts	_____	_____
_____	Flextime	_____	_____
_____	Paid Holidays	_____	_____
_____	Life and Disability Insurance	_____	_____
_____	Medical Insurance	_____	_____
_____	Paid Time Off	_____	_____
_____	Relocation Expenses	_____	_____
_____	Retirement	_____	_____
_____	Signing Bonus	_____	_____
_____	Stock Purchase or Savings Plan	_____	_____
_____	Telecommuting Options	_____	_____
_____	Tuition Assistance	_____	_____
_____	Paid Vacation Days	_____	_____
_____	Wellness Programs	_____	_____
_____		_____	_____

For more information on each benefit, visit the **www.YourStepsTowardSuccess.com** website.

Selecting the Best Offer

Purpose

The purpose of this lesson is to help you strategically select the best job offer.

Objectives

Check each objective upon completion.

❑ Explain how to strategically identify the best job offer.

❑ Discuss the three options for responding to a job offer.

Identifying the Best Offer

After you have submitted winning résumés and cover letters and interviewed successfully, you may be offered numerous employment opportunities. How do you decide which opportunity to accept?

To begin evaluating your job offers, make a list of all of the features that are important to you. Such features could include the organization's reputation/prestige, job functions, training program, salary, benefits, job location, opportunity for advancement, work environment, opportunity for free time (evenings and weekends), opportunity for travel, colleagues with whom you'll be working, on-site fitness center, tuition reimbursement, etc.

Three Job Offer Options

Once you have been offered a job, you have three options:

1. **Delay Your Response**: As soon as you receive the offer, you need to express appreciation for the offer and let the employer know that you will think carefully about the offer. To be respectful, you need to provide the employer an answer within five days.

2. **Accept the Offer**: Show your appreciation for the offer and ask the employer to confirm the offer in writing.

3. **Reject the Offer**: Express your appreciation for the offer and for the company's confidence. State something positive about the employer and be diplomatic before you decline the offer.

Once you have made your list of features, rank the features in order of importance. After ranking the features, create a system to analyze your offers. You may want to use a system similar to the following:

Your Priority	Feature	Offer #1	Offer #2	Offer #3	Offer #4
10	Co-Workers/Work Environment	2	2	2	2
2	Job Functions	2	1	2	1
1	Management Style	2	1	1	1
3	Salary and Benefits	3	2	2	2
7	The Organization	1	2	1	2
5	Location / Commute	4	1	4	2
4	Organizational Flexibility	3	2	2	2
6	Opportunity to Travel	4	1	3	3
9	Opportunity for Continuing Education / Training	3	1	4	2
8	Opportunity for Advancement	3	1	2	2
11	On-Site or Close Fitness Center	4	4	3	2
Total		31	18	26	21

1 = Excellent   2 = Good   3 = Fair   4 = Poor

If the table above represented your job offers, then you would want to accept Job Offer #2.

Use the following table when evaluating your job offers:

Offer #1: _____

Offer #2: _____

Offer #3: _____

Offer #4: _____

Your Priority	Feature	Offer #1	Offer #2	Offer #3	Offer #4
Total					

1 = Excellent	2 = Good	3 = Fair	4 = Poor

Which offer are you going to accept?

_____

_____

_____

Summary

Once you have completed the following and obtained a job, then you are ready to advance in your career:

❑ Identified what job search methods you were going to use to search for employment

❑ Determined whom you were going to contact about employment opportunities

❑ Created a network file

❑ Completed the résumé research questions

❑ Drafted and formatted a general résumé

❑ Drafted and formatted a general cover letter

❑ Created an electronic version of your résumé and cover letter

❑ Developed a career portfolio

❑ Prepared answers to the common interview questions

❑ Conducted a mock interview

❑ Drafted a general thank you letter

❑ Researched your salary requirements

❑ Determined the benefits you needed versus the benefits you wanted

❑ Identified your best job offer

❑ Accepted a job offer

ADVANCING IN YOUR CAREER

Beginning Your New Job

Purpose

The purpose of this lesson is to discuss the ways you can make a good impression when you begin your new job.

Objectives

Check each objective upon completion.

❑ Discuss the guidelines for making a good first impression.

❑ Explain cubicle etiquette.

Making a Good Impression and Succeeding in Your Career

First impressions always form the basis of the way people view you. It is extremely important to make a good first impression as you begin your new job. Use the following guidelines to succeed in your career:

- Always be thinking about how to complete a task more effectively

- Be flexible

- Be honest

- Be humble and teachable

- Be on time

- Be polite

- Be professional

- Communicate openly and clearly

- Continue to learn

- Demonstrate and document your value

- Dress appropriately (observe your superiors' dress)

- Keep an open mind

- Learn the organization's culture

- Look for leadership opportunities

- Observe your co-workers

- Perform your tasks well and on time

- Respect everyone, including secretaries, security guards, and maintenance personnel

- Share your ideas

- Welcome change

- Work smarter, harder, and faster

To make a good impression and succeed in your career, it is important that you dress appropriately for the job you are performing. Some professions have uniforms, but most professions allow you to choose the type of clothing you wear to work. Whatever the dress standard is for the occupation you have chosen, your clothes need to be clean and pressed and your shoes need to be clean and polished.

A good guideline to follow is to dress for the job you want and not the job you have. It is better to be over-dressed then it is to be under-dressed. How you dress in the business world will impact your upward mobility in your career. You need to dress for success!

Cubicle Etiquette

Almost all employees begin their careers working in a cubicle. Most cubicles come with a desk, telephone, computer, chair, and filing cabinet. Since you'll spend more than 2,000 hours a year in your cubicle it is important that you customize your "home away from home." As you decorate your cubicle keep in mind that your cubicle was designed as a workspace and your decorations should not distract you from your work. Follow these basic guidelines to decorate appropriately:

- Take hints about appropriate decorations from your superiors' offices

- Determine who is going to see your cubicle

- Use welcoming decorations, like nicely-framed family pictures, diplomas, or inspirational photographs

- Don't use distracting or inappropriate decorations

- Be professional in decorating

Since cubicles are so close together, there is a noticeable lack of privacy. Your co-workers can see, hear, and smell your cubicle. Follow these basic rules for general cubicle etiquette:

- Gently knock on the side cubicle wall when you approach an individual's cubicle

- Use a soft voice while on the phone or when meeting in your cubicle

- Do not use a speakerphone

- Wear headphones if you listen to music

- Be aware of your habits (humming, cracking your knuckles, chomping ice, etc.)

- Do not wear a lot of perfume or cologne

- Do not take off your shoes

- Do not eat pungent foods

- Do not take anything from anyone else's cubicle

- Do not glance in other's cubicles

Effective Communication

Purpose

The purpose of this lesson is to teach you how to effectively communicate in a workplace environment. Effective communication is the key to success. You must learn how to communicate if you want to succeed and progress in your career.

Objectives

Check each objective upon completion.

❑ Describe the techniques for effective communication.

❑ Explain the importance of using "I" statements.

❑ Describe the types of nonverbal behavior.

❑ Explain the techniques for active listening.

Effective Communication Techniques

Communication is effective when the perceived message matches the intended message. You will be more likely to achieve this match if you do the following:

- **Understand your intention**

    Since the communication process begins with an intended message, you need to be clear about what you want to say before you begin speaking.

- **Say what you mean**

    When you say something that doesn't match your intention, your message will confuse the other person. If you are having trouble finding the words to express your intention, try saying something like, "I'm having trouble figuring out how to say this."

- **Listen for content, feeling, and intent**

    Our work culture discourages us from explicitly communicating and acknowledging feelings. Yet, feelings are important factors in work situations so we must actively seek to understand them. In addition, we must seek to understand each other's intentions, because no matter what words we use, it's the intention that really matters.

- **Check for understanding**

    Communication often breaks down because people make assumptions, or because they assume they understand when they don't. You must be an active listener to understand—ask questions, paraphrase, and summarize to clarify your understanding.

- **Use "I" statements**

    "I" statements describe your ideas and feelings. "You" statements carry a judgmental tone, which puts the other person on the defensive.

Using "I" Statements

There are two different types of statements – "I" statements and "You" statements.

"I" statements tend to:

- Place responsibility with you, the speaker
- Clarify your position, feelings, or opinions
- Build trust by giving others information about yourself

"You" statements tend to:

- Put people down
- Place blame
- Preach about how other people should work, think, or feel
- Result in a negative or defensive response

Examples of "I" Statements	Examples of "You" Statements
I couldn't understand what you said.	You aren't making any sense.
I missed having your input at the team meeting.	You didn't care enough to come to the meeting.
I'm worried about meeting the deadline.	You won't be able to make the deadline.

Nonverbal Messages

When you convey your intentions, you use both verbal and nonverbal behaviors. When there is congruence between verbal and nonverbal cues, the message is strengthened. When there is incongruence, people respond to the nonverbal message and disregard the verbal content. Therefore, when you listen to someone else, you need to listen with your eyes as well as your ears. Similarly, you need to use nonverbal behaviors that convey your intentions. These are some common types of nonverbal behaviors:

Vocal Characteristics:	Tone, pitch, tempo, pace, volume, etc.
Facial Expressions:	Smile, frown, surprise, etc.
Body Posture, Movement and Gestures:	Shoulder shrug, slouching, folding arms, etc.
Use of Space:	How close, how far, leaning toward, moving away, etc.

Active Listening Techniques

Active listening is a key to communicating effectively. The following active listening techniques can assist you in improving your ability to communicate:

Remove Distractions:	Eliminate background noise, such as the television or radio
Listen:	Listen for content, intention, and feelings of the person with whom you are talking
Pay Attention to Nonverbal Cues:	Notice the person's body language
Demonstrate Responsiveness:	Maintain eye contact and ask questions to clarify and confirm your understanding
Check for Understanding:	Paraphrase what you heard

Frequent and consistent use of the active listening techniques above will greatly enhance your ability to communicate effectively.

Activity—One-Way Versus Two-Way Communication

Purpose

The purpose of this activity is to help you apply effective communication techniques.

Process

- Ask a family member or friend to participate in this activity with you.
- Provide the person with two blank pieces of paper and a pen or pencil.

One-Way Communication Exercise

- Sit back-to-back with the individual you asked to participate.
- Explain to this person that his or her task is to simply follow your instructions and sketch the diagram you are going to describe. Explain that he or she **cannot** ask any questions.
- Describe diagram 1 (seen on the next page). Make sure he or she cannot see the diagram.
- After you have finished describing the diagram, turn around and look at what the person drew. How similar is it to the diagram you were explaining? Ask him or her how he or she felt when you were explaining the diagram. Did he or she want to ask questions? Was it difficult for both of you to only have one-way communication?

Two-Way Communication Exercise Using Effective Communications Techniques

- Sit facing the person you asked to participate.
- Explain that his or her task is to follow your instructions and sketch the diagram you are going to explain. Let the person know that he or she **can** ask questions.
- Describe diagram 2 (seen on the next page). Even though you are facing each other, make sure he or she cannot see the diagram.
- After you have finished describing the diagram, look at what the person drew. How similar is it to the diagram you were explaining? Ask the person how he or she felt when you were explaining the diagram. Did he or she feel that he or she was able to draw the diagram because he or she was able to ask questions?

One-Way Versus Two-Way Communication

- Debrief the activity with the individual who participated.

Two-way communication allows both parties to understand each other. Practice using the techniques you learned in this lesson to become an effective communicator.

Diagram 1:

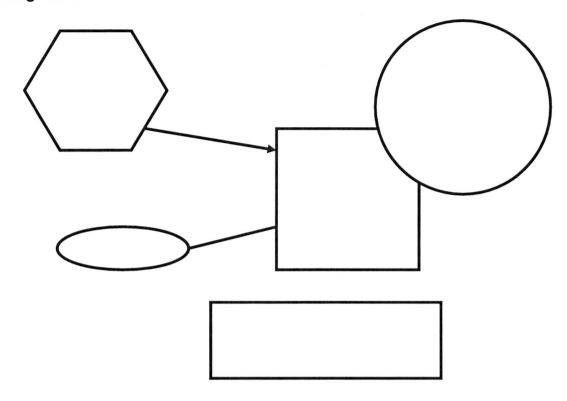

Diagram 2:

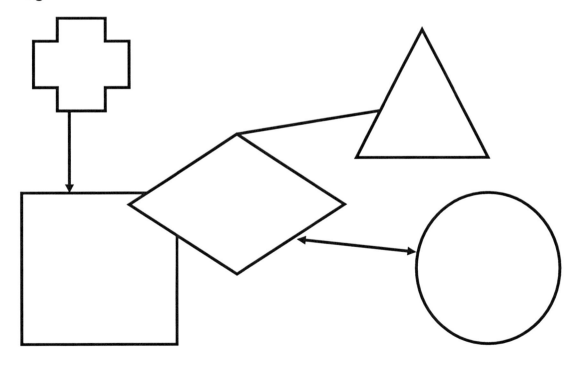

Business Ethics

Purpose

The purpose of this lesson is to define ethics and how to handle an ethical dilemma.

Objectives

Check each objective upon completion.

❑ Define ethics.

❑ Explain the difference between ethics and values.

❑ Describe the questions you should ask yourself when faced with an ethical dilemma.

Ethics

Every employee should know about ethics, so that he or she is prepared to face ethical dilemmas on the job.

So what are ethics?

Webster's Dictionary[9] defines ethics as:
- The discipline dealing with what is good and bad and with moral duty and obligation
- A set of moral principles or values
- A theory or system of moral values
- The principles of conduct governing an individual or a group (professional ethics)
- A guiding philosophy

In summary, ethics are standards of conduct that guide decisions and actions.

Values

Our values should impact our ethics. So what are values?

Frank Navran[10], the Ethics Research Center's Principal Consultant, states "Values are our fundamental beliefs or principles. They define what we think is right, good, fair, and just. Ethics are behaviors and tell people how to act in ways that meet the standard our values set for us."

Jennifer J. Salopek[11], an author and writer for business magazines, explains further, "It's not the company's place to tell you what your values ought to be; they come with you when you enter the workplace. But it is the company's responsibility to set behavioral standards and its obligation to train employees in what those standards are."

In summary, values are an individual's fundamental beliefs or principles.

In the workplace, it is critical that you are honest and make good choices so that you develop a reputation as an ethical individual.

Questions for an Ethical Dilemma

No matter how ethical you are, you will be faced with ethical dilemmas. It is important that you ask yourself the right questions to determine your next action. Dayton Fandray[12], writer and editor, described a tool called the Ethics Quick Test. It asks employees to consider these questions when faced with ethical dilemmas:

- Is the action legal?
- Is it right?
- Does it fit the company's values?
- Will it reflect poorly on the company?
- How will it make you feel about yourself?
- How do others feel about it?
- How would you feel if the whole world knew about it?
- Does the behavior make sense?
- Is the situation fair to everyone involved?
- Will the people in authority at your organization approve?
- How would you feel if someone did the same thing to you?
- Will something bad happen if you don't make a decision?

Activity—What Should You Do?

Purpose

The purpose of this activity is to allow you time to determine what you would do if you were faced with an ethical dilemma.

Process

- Read each situation.

- Ask yourself the questions on the previous page.

- Prepare a brief written response for each situation.

Situation One

According to your company's policy, quality is the highest priority. You are working on a rush order and have cut some corners in order to meet the deadline. It would take at least another day to do a quality job, but then you would miss the deadline and both the customer and your boss would be unhappy. What should you do?

_____

_____

_____

_____

_____

_____

_____

_____

_____

_____

_____

_____

_____

_____

_____

_____

_____

Situation Two

A fellow employee is being harassed at work and is afraid to say or do anything about it for fear of losing her job. You have witnessed several instances of the harassment, and you also fear retaliation from the company if you blow the whistle. You can't afford to lose your job either. What should you do?

_____

_____

_____

_____

_____

_____

_____

_____

_____

Situation Three

One of your co-workers, who is also a personal friend, has been going through a number of health and personal problems, and has used all of his sick time. You have tried to be a good listener, and to help out when you can. Now your co-worker has asked you to punch in for him and cover for him during a medical appointment. What should you do?

_____

_____

_____

_____

_____

_____

_____

_____

_____

Situation Four

You have discovered an error made by your department that may compromise and delay the production process. The error is small, but you can't determine what the effects on the final product might be. If you report the error, your department will look bad, and you might even lose part of your profit sharing for the quarter. What should you do?

_____

_____

_____

_____

_____

_____

_____

_____

_____

_____

Summary

Once you have completed the following and advanced in your career, then you are ready to lead a team to success:

- ❑ Understand how to make a good impression

- ❑ Understand office and cubicle etiquette

- ❑ Become an effective communicator

- ❑ Become an ethical employee

LEADING YOUR
TEAM TO SUCCESS

Transition from Management to Leadership

Purpose

Your title may be Manager, Team Leader, Supervisor, or even Director. Regardless of your title, if you are responsible for the performance of other individuals then you need to be a leader!

"Manager" is a leadership title, but leadership is a much broader concept and brings with it a broader scope of responsibilities. You must have the desire and persistence to become a leader.

The purpose of this lesson is to identify how to make the transition from management to leadership.

Objectives

Check each objective upon completion.

- ❑ Discuss the term "management" and the attributes and roles of a manager.

- ❑ Discuss the term "leadership" and the attributes and roles of a leader.

- ❑ Compare the characteristics of management and leadership.

- ❑ Describe the benefits of leadership.

Management

Management is defined as effectively utilizing and organizing resources (employees, money, equipment, processes, etc.) to accomplish goals.

Managers have numerous attributes and roles. Some of the attributes and roles of a manager are contained in the table below:

Attribute or Role	Definition
Autocratic	Being absolute
Budgeting	Allocating funds according to the needs of the business
Constant	Being invariable or unchanging
Controlling	Exercising direct influence over others
Firm	Solidly fixed in place
Organizing	Arranging by systematic planning and united effort
Planning	Creating a detailed formulation of a program of action
Problem Solving	Finding a solution, explanation, or answer for a situation
Staffing	Hiring individuals to assist with the operations of a business
Training	Teaching so as to make fit, qualified, or proficient

What other attributes or roles do you associate with managers?

_____

_____

_____

_____

_____

_____

_____

Leadership

Leadership is defined as the ability to influence people to move toward a common goal.

Leaders also have numerous attributes and roles. Some of the attributes and roles of a leader are contained in the table below:

Attribute or Role	Definition
Align people	Positioning people in line with one another
Emphasize systems and practices that are proactive	Acting in anticipation of future systems or practices
Emphasize the positive impact of a team member	Recognizing a team member who has contributed to the goal of the organization
Empower others	Promoting the self-actualization or influence of others
Establish direction	Providing guidance of actions
Generate new ideas	Creating a visible representation of a conception
Motivate others	Causing people to act
To be team oriented and results oriented	Focusing on team members and work product results
Think of ways to utilize each team member's strengths	Identifying the ability of each team member to contribute to the team
Use creativity to complete projects and solve problems	Creating solutions
View the organization as a dynamic system	Providing the organization and team with the ability to progress

From your experience, what other attributes or roles does a leader possess?

_____

_____

_____

_____

_____

_____

_____

Activity—Identifying Characteristics

Purpose

The purpose of this activity is to identify the different characteristics of leadership and management.

Process

- Using the game board on the following page, read and place the following statements under the appropriate heading (Leadership or Management).

Achieves Goals

Asks Questions

Creates a Vision

Directs Others

Focuses on Bottom Line

Focuses on the Process

Follows Orders

Identifies Opportunities

Inspires Others

Likes Control

Maintains Current Responsibilities

Manages Change

Motivates Others

Sets Goals

Takes Few Risks

Takes Risks

Uses Creativity

Uses Formal Solutions

Leadership	Management

Note: The answer key is located on page 170. The first purpose of this activity is to identify the characteristics of leadership and management. The second purpose is to help you realize that leadership and management characteristics are closely linked. Even though you may feel confused during this activity, do your best to complete the activity.

Leadership versus Management

What is the difference between management and leadership? First, leaders create a vision and strategize how to help their teams achieve the vision. Managers create a step by step plan to meet the deadline, and they budget the time and finances to achieve the goal. An effective manager is both a leader and a manager. An effective leader, on the other hand, does not need to be in a management position to positively influence a team.

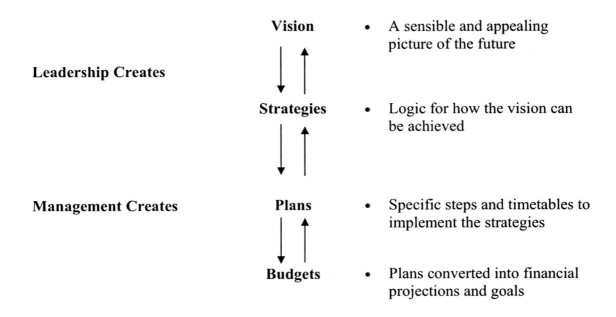

Leadership Creates

Vision
- A sensible and appealing picture of the future

Strategies
- Logic for how the vision can be achieved

Management Creates

Plans
- Specific steps and timetables to implement the strategies

Budgets
- Plans converted into financial projections and goals

Activity—Identifying Responsibilities

Purpose

The purpose of this activity is to identify the various leadership and management responsibilities you have and to help you determine the differences and similarities between these responsibilities.

Process

- Identify responsibilities you currently have as a manager, supervisor, or team leader.

- Determine which tasks within the identified responsibilities are considered leadership tasks and which tasks are considered management tasks.

- Propose what you can do differently to function more as a leader or more as a manager.

What are the responsibilities you currently have as a manager, supervisor, or team leader?

_____

_____

_____

_____

Which tasks are considered leadership tasks?

Leadership: _____

_____

_____

Which tasks are considered management tasks?

Management: _____

_____

_____

What can you do differently to function more as a leader or more as a manager?

Leader: _____

_____

Manager: _____

_____

_____

_____

Notes:

_____

_____

_____

_____

_____

_____

_____

_____

_____

_____

Benefits of Leadership

Leadership offers many benefits. You have the opportunity to be a leader throughout your career whether or not you are in management positions.

What are the benefits of leadership?

_____

_____

_____

_____

_____

_____

_____

What do you admire about good leaders you know?

_____

_____

_____

_____

_____

_____

_____

What type of positive impact have you experienced from a good leader?

_____

_____

_____

_____

_____

_____

_____

When you are in a leadership position, be sure to remember the qualities that good leaders possess. Apply those skills and empower your team members to achieve their goals!

Motivation

Purpose

The purpose of this lesson is to explain the importance of understanding the principles of motivation and how to increase each team member's motivation.

Objectives

Check each objective upon completion.

- ❑ Explain motivation and how to motivate your team members.

- ❑ Discuss the four predominant motivation theories:

    - ❑ Maintenance-Motivation Theory

    - ❑ Affiliation, Achievement, Power

    - ❑ Growth, Relatedness, Existence

    - ❑ Maslow's Hierarchy of Needs

- ❑ Describe the synthesis of the four theories.

- ❑ Identify potential motivating solutions.

Motivation Overview

Motivation is what makes people direct their behavior toward achieving a goal. Everyone has certain needs, and everyone is motivated by a desire to fulfill those needs.

Since we are all different, we all have different needs, and are motivated by different things. One mistake many leaders make is assuming that others are motivated by the same things that motivate them. Rather, part of your job is to listen to the individuals on your team and learn what motivates each member of your team.

To motivate your team members you need to:

1. Recognize that each of your team members has individual differences;

2. Match your team members to jobs that they enjoy and are motivated to complete;

3. Set appropriate goals according to each team member's motivations;

4. Ensure that goals are perceived as attainable by every team member;

5. Individualize rewards according to each team member's desires;

6. Link rewards to performance; and

7. Check the reward system for equality.

Four Predominant Motivation Theories

A number of social scientists have developed theories on motivation that have been applied to the workplace. The motivational theories included in this lesson will help you better understand what influences people to do what they do and will help you lead people to reach their personal goals and the organization's goals.

Maintenance Factors vs. Motivation Factors

Psychologist Frederick Herzberg[13] asked workers what made them unhappy or dissatisfied and what made them happy or satisfied with their jobs. He concluded that people have two distinct categories of needs that are independent of each other and affect behavior in different ways. He called the categories **maintenance** and **motivation**.

Put simply, maintenance factors are seen as part of the job, and will not motivate people. The absence of maintenance factors can limit performance, but their presence alone will not improve performance.

Maintenance factors include:

- Policies and Administrative Practices
- Supervision
- Working Conditions
- Interpersonal Relations
- Salary and Other Compensation
- Status
- Job Security

Motivation factors, on the other hand, push people to superior performance. They promote increased productivity, create a stimulating place to work, and provide true personal job satisfaction.

Motivation factors include the following:

- Recognition
- Achievement
- Stimulating or Interesting Work
- Responsibility
- Advancement
- Growth

Affiliation, Achievement, Power

According to Dr. David C. McClelland[14] people have a need for **affiliation**, **achievement**, or **power**:

Affiliation: Individuals motivated by affiliation need to have associates, team relationships, and feelings of belonging.

> *Team members who have a high need for affiliation meet this need through teamwork and group tasks. They like an environment in which they can talk with, or be physically surrounded by, others.*

Achievement: Individuals motivated by achievement need to produce results, meet high but realistic standards, master difficult tasks, and perform better than others.

> *Team members with a high need for achievement set challenging goals for themselves and respond well when others expect a high level of performance from them. They enjoy change, risk-taking, and either working independently or working with equally competent people.*

Power: Individuals motivated by power need to extend personal control or influence over other people, events or situations.

> *Team members can meet their power needs at work by leading meetings, making presentations, chairing committees, writing procedures, managing supplies, or making decisions that affect others.*

Growth, Relatedness, Existence

Dr. Clayton P. Alderfer[15] has proposed three core human needs. These three needs are **growth**, **relatedness**, and **existence**.

Growth: Personal growth in one's job; this includes increased responsibilities, broader scope of tasks, greater room for creativity, learning new skills and abilities, building new relationships with colleagues, and upward and lateral mobility through the organization.

Relatedness: A feeling of connectedness to co-workers and colleagues through relationships and teamwork; a feeling that an individual is part of a greater whole (the team or the organization).

Existence: Conducting work that is personally meaningful in some way; understanding that the work one does may serve a greater purpose and may reach a broader scope than one's own immediate area; justifying one's own existence through the work one performs.

Hierarchy of Needs

Abraham Maslow[16] is known for establishing the theory of a **Hierarchy of Needs**. He wrote that human beings are motivated by unsatisfied needs, and that certain lower needs have to be satisfied before higher needs can be satisfied.

Need	Description
Physiological	Being able to meet and sustain one's need for food, air, water, and any special health needs (i.e., medical conditions, etc.) in the work environment.
Safety	Being able to meet and sustain one's need to be physically and emotionally safe in the work environment.
Social	The need to interact with co-workers, colleagues, and friends in the work environment; feeling connected to others.
Esteem	The need to feel a sense of accomplishment in the work one does; conducting work that is personally meaningful and gratifying.
Self-Actualization	The need to reach one's highest potential in the work one does and within one's organization.

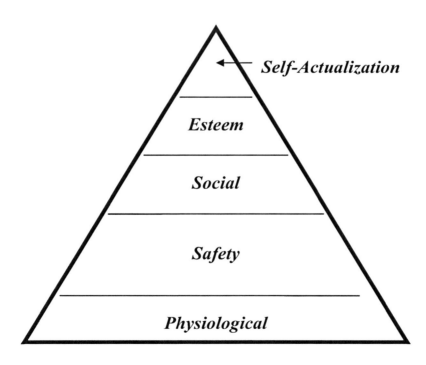

Synthesis of Four Motivation Theories

Paul Hersey, Ken Blanchard, and Dewey Johnson introduced a synthesis of these four popular motivation theories. Their goal was to provide a simple, useful categorization of the following three primary areas of motivation that drive individuals:

- **People Seek Security**

    There are certain security needs fundamental to peoples' existence, like receiving a paycheck. If your team members security needs are not addressed, they will not put their main focus on job performance. We cannot neglect the security aspect of effective organizations.

- **People Seek Social Systems**

    Whether we call this need relatedness, affiliation, interpersonal relations, or belonging, we cannot neglect the importance of camaraderie in effective organizations.

- **People Seek Personal Growth**

    Whether we call this self-actualization, advancement, growth, or need for achievement, "what's in it for me" is a powerful need. We cannot neglect the development aspect of effective organizations.

Potential Motivating Solutions

There are a variety of ways to motivate your team members. Below are some examples of motivation strategies:

- **The Work Itself**

  Some team members are motivated by the actual work they do. As his or her leader, take the time to find out what specifically it is about the work that motivates each team member (e.g., solving problems, public speaking, writing reports, etc.). Then, continue to build these specific motivating tasks into his or her work as much as possible.

- **Money**

  Research indicates that money can make up as much as 50-60% of an individual's overall motivation. However, research also suggests money alone cannot motivate—it's what the money gives a person (possessions, free time, status, etc.). If you have the ability to reward team members with money, it is a useful strategy.

- **Flextime / Flexiplace**

  Allowing team members the autonomy to work at home or hold non-traditional hours in the office can be seen as extremely valuable, as people put a high value on internal control.

- **Recognition**

  Formally and informally recognizing team member achievements is a necessity. This ranges from a simple "thank you" to formal recognition in front of peers (e.g., public awards, praise during a team meeting, etc.). Various forms of feedback can be used.

- **Growth Opportunities**

  Training, special job assignments, special projects, cross training, and volunteering provide team members with growth opportunities.

- **Social Outlets**

  Having office gatherings occasionally, after-work functions, or simply allowing for open dialogue at work can be viable motivators.

- **Leader Attitude**

  Your attitude as a leader, the way you treat your team members, and the energy you exude are all strong motivators. These are factors that make people want to follow your lead. Remember, you cannot motivate another person; you can only create opportunities for others to be self-motivated!

Activity—Recognizing Team Members' Motivational Needs

Purpose

The purpose of this activity is to identify various motivational techniques for each of your team members.

Process

- Identify your team members.

- Describe the team members' motivation levels.

- Think about the strategies for increasing the chosen team members' motivation based on the motivation theories and potential solutions.

- Generate a list of motivating solutions. For example, if a team member seeks "social systems," then what can you and your organization do to meet this need? (You could hold staff meetings, staff parties, or other social events.)

  Note: Use the list of *Potential Motivating Solutions* to assist you in generating your own list.

Team Member Name and Motivation Level	Motivating Solutions

Foundations of Teamwork

Purpose

The purpose of this lesson is to provide you with the essential foundation and concepts of teamwork.

Objectives

Check each objective upon completion.

- ❑ Define a work group.

- ❑ Define a team.

- ❑ Discuss the differences between a work group and a team.

- ❑ Describe the four stages of team development:

- ❑ Explain the practices of an effective team.

- ❑ Describe the group attributes of an effective team.

Work Group

A work group focuses on individual work products. While each product is primarily the result of one individual, a work group consists of several individuals working on separate, but related, work products.

Team

A team is a small number of people, with complementary skills, who are committed to a common purpose for which they hold themselves mutually accountable[17]. Therefore, the essence of a team is common commitment. Without this commitment, groups perform as individuals; with it, they become a powerful unit of collective performance.

Work Group versus Team

The following table outlines the differences between work groups and teams:

Work Group	Team
Strong leadership	Shared leadership
Individual accountability	Mutual accountability
Purpose defined by management	Purpose developed by team input
Individual work products	Collective work products
Meetings tend to be one-way or informational	Meetings tend to involve participation and problem solving
Effectiveness is measured mainly by others in the organization	Effectiveness is measured by both the team and others in the organization
Decisions made by one expert, leader, or majority vote	Decisions made by reaching a consensus

Stages of Team Development

There are four stages of team development:

- Forming
- Storming
- Norming
- Performing

These stages mark the process of a developing team, and the following table describes each stage of team development[18].

Stage	Description
Forming	During the Forming stage, the team first comes together to form a team. The team members may be cautious and are focused on defining the boundaries and roles. During this stage, the business goals are sidetracked.
Storming	During the Storming stage, conflict among team members may be exhibited. The conflict usually includes power struggles with a further defining of roles. The team may experience frustration, discouragement, and low morale. It is necessary to go through this stage to grow as a team.
Norming	During the Norming stage, the group begins to establish guidelines (norms) for how they will work together. Each team member is comfortable with his or her role and tasks. The team begins to move toward focusing on business goals.
Performing	During the Performing stage, a true team begins to work well together to achieve business goals. Each team member feels competence, commitment and confidence with his or her team because the team is now comfortable supporting each other and handling conflict.

Effective Team Practices

Have you ever wondered why some teams accomplish their goals while other teams do not accomplish their goals?

Since you want to be the leader of a successful team, learn to apply the following practices:

Best Practice	Description
Gathering	The first practice used to build a high-performance team is to gather information about your team. You must understand the talents and needs of each team member in order to provide each team member with the appropriate responsibilities. It is also important to gather answers to important questions, such as: • What is the vision for the team? • What is the strategy to fulfill the vision? • What information do we need to complete this project? • What methods or ideas are most effective and efficient in completing this project? • What resources are needed? • How can each team member contribute? • Does every team member understand the details of the project? • What is the timeline for the project?
Creating	You and your team must be creative. You must find the most effective and efficient method of accomplishing a task. You must also create a strategy to fulfill the vision of the team.
Designing	After creating the most effective and efficient method to accomplish a task, your team must ensure the methods are practical. This ensures that your team's plan is realistic.
Selling	As a team, you must sell your ideas and support your strategy to other individuals in order to obtain the necessary resources to complete the task. A highly effectively team works together to sell its ideas.
Communicating	Once you have received the appropriate resources, the project goals and the expectations of each team member needs to be communicated. Throughout the project, each team member should have open communication with the others.

Best Practice	Description
Reviewing	Throughout the project's development, the team should continually review the methods they are using and the focus of the project in order to produce the desired outcomes. The team should also review the issues that may be hindering the team's ability to accomplish their goals.
Collaborating	All team members need to work together to accomplish the desired outcome. It is important that all team members understand that they must work together as a team. As a team, they need to address the hindering issues, remove the inhibitors, and continue working to achieve the team goals.
Delivering	Once each team member has taken action and fulfilled the expectations set for him or her, the team should deliver the final product together as a team.

Effective Team Attributes

Effective teams have certain attributes that contribute to their effectiveness. The following is a list of some attributes of an effective team:

Attribute or Role	Definition
Shared Vision / Common Goal	A vision or goal is shared by all members of a group
Integrity	A firm adherence to a code of moral values
Confidence and Trust	A feeling of assured reliance on the character, ability, strength, or truth of someone or something
Collaboration	To work jointly with others
Encouragement	To inspire with courage, spirit, or hope

What attributes of effective teams have you observed?

_____

_____

_____

What attributes do you, as a leader of a team, need to establish within your team?

_____

_____

Team Building

Purpose

The purpose of this lesson is to explain the concepts and methods essential for team leaders to be effective in enhancing team cohesion.

Objectives

Check each objective upon completion.

☐ Define the goals of team building.

☐ Explain the various formal methods of team building.

☐ Explain the various informal methods of team building.

☐ Describe how to increase team performance through communication, trust, and shared work.

Team Building Goals

To develop a strong, effective team you must understand the goals of team building.

A team develops when there is a legitimate business reason for people to work together as a team, such as a common project, work product, or business goal. Once the team has been developed, it must be trained. Basic team training should be provided to help team members understand the foundations for working effectively as a team.

Finally, there must be management support and organizational commitment to implement change and do what is required to make the team successful. Once the team is developed, trained, and supported, it is time to institute the following team building goals:

Goal	Action Plan
Enhanced Communication	Team members must learn effective two-way communication skills, each team member's communication style, and how to effectively interact with each other.
Enhanced Trust	Since team members rely on each other to reach a common goal, there must be a level of trust between them. Trust is built over time. It is important for team members to learn effective conflict management strategies to build and maintain trust. If trust is lost, it is difficult to regain.
Increased Cohesion	Once communication and trust are enhanced, team cohesion (a sense of feeling connected among team members) follows. It is important to recognize when cohesion is high or low. This can usually be determined by the amount of communication, cooperation, and work produced by a team.
Increased Production	The business goal of team building is increased production of quality work products.

Formal Team Building Methods

Formal methods of team building include the following:

- Structured workplace meetings with the goal of enhancing team cohesiveness, such as communication, trust, resolution of conflict issues, etc. Often, these meetings are facilitated by a trained, third-party, objective professional.

- Off-site retreats where the goal is to work on one or several team goals. These can be held at hotels, wilderness camps, restaurants, or other off-site locations.

What could you do to hold a formal team building activity?

_____

_____

_____

_____

_____

_____

Informal Team Building Methods

Informal methods of team building are virtually unlimited. Informal team building methods have two factors in common—focusing on daily workplace interactions and achieving work product goals. Examples may include breakfast bagels every Friday to talk about the tasks for the upcoming week, or a lunch each month to evaluate the team's progress on a project.

What are some more examples of informal team building methods?

_____

_____

_____

_____

_____

_____

_____

_____

_____

_____

_____

_____

Increase Team Performance

As a leader, you want to build a productive team and increase your team's performance. You can increase your team's performance through enhancing communication, sharing trust and sharing work. Below are some recommended strategies to enhance communication and trust between team members:

Strategy	Details
Enhancing Communication	
Regular Team Meetings	Business or team meetings that are held regularly allow team members to communicate about various issues.
	Team communication is enhanced as a byproduct of meeting regularly.
	The key to enhancing communication is to have consistent, ongoing opportunities for team members to be together and interact.
Leader's Communication Style	The team leader, manager, or supervisor of the team must use an open, two-way communication style. This facilitates open communication among team members and enhances their opportunities to interact more effectively with each other.
	As the leader, you set the tone for the team, so your open communication style is important.
Sharing Trust	
No Gossip Rule	Gossip in the workplace is often damaging to team spirit because it innately pits two or more people against each other. Make a team rule to avoid gossiping about each other and stick to professional matters in the workplace. Eliminating the appearance of gossip, whether perceived or real, will assist with enhancing, repairing, and maintaining trust among team members.
The Follow-Through Rule	Trust is built when team members do what they say they will do. Team members realize they can count on one another when they exhibit follow-through.
	To implement this rule, allow team members to know who is assigned to each task. This practice will begin to foster mutual accountability among team members.

Strategy	Details
Sharing Work	
Communication and Trust Enhancement	Communication and trust will be naturally enhanced when team members are tasked with meeting a common goal and are required to work together to reach the common goal.
Collaboration Efforts	Allow team members to work together. More than likely the project will be accomplished faster.
Team Member Empowerment	Shared work allows team members to feel empowered, excited, involved, and proud of their work because they completed the project as a team.

How are you going to increase your team's performance?

_____

_____

_____

_____

_____

_____

_____

_____

_____

_____

_____

_____

_____

_____

_____

_____

_____

_____

_____

_____

_____

_____

_____

Situational Leadership

Purpose

The purpose of this lesson is to introduce you to the Situational Leadership model as a means of adapting your leadership style to effectively work with each of your team members.

Objectives

Check each objective upon completion.

- ❏ Explain the Situational Leadership model.

- ❏ Discuss the four different styles of leadership.

- ❏ Describe the four levels of employee readiness.

- ❏ Discuss which leadership style will meet each team member's readiness needs.

Situational Leadership Style

Over the last few decades, people in the management field have been searching for a "best" style of leadership. However, the evidence from research clearly indicates that there is no single all-purpose leadership style. Instead successful leaders adapt their behavior to meet the demands of their unique situations. This adaptation of behavior is called Situational Leadership.

In your job, the demands may change rapidly and you may be confused about the way you should act. Situational leadership can help you make rational choices about when to use a certain style of leadership.

The Situational Leadership model helps you to develop the following:

Diagnostic Skills: The ability to determine the level of "readiness" an employee (or a group of employees) exhibits on a specific task, function, activity, or objective.

Adaptive Skills: The ability to vary the amount of direction (task behavior) you provide, and the amount of social and emotional support (relationship behavior) you provide.

Four Leadership Styles

Situational leadership is the result of extensive research to determine the best style of leadership to use when leading employees. As a result of the research, four best styles of leadership were identified that can help you lead your team members.

The four leadership styles are as follows:

- Directing
- Supporting
- Participating
- Delegating

The problem many leaders have is using the wrong leadership style for a team member or using the same leadership style for all team members. Using the *right* leadership style with each team member is an effective way to foster teamwork.

Use the following table to learn about the four leadership styles:

Style	Description	Works well with...
Directing	The leader provides a high level of task behavior and lesser amounts of relationship behavior.	Team members who require a lot of direction in learning/doing a task. Often, this is the case when a team member is new to the job or a particular task. However, remember that most team members and teams want to learn their job and get it done with minimal supervision—they want to be autonomous.
Supporting	The leader provides high levels of both task and relationship behavior. In essence, the leader provides a combination of direction and encouragement related to accomplishing the task.	Team members who require direction on completing a task, as well as motivation or encouragement regarding any insecurity about accomplishing a task.
Participating	The leader provides high levels of relationship behavior and lower levels of task direction.	Team members who are skilled at performing the task at hand, but lack motivation in doing the task. The leader uses the participating style to provide the team member with active, personal participation in getting the task done. When the leader directly participates in completing the task and provides encouragement, the team member is more likely to be motivated to accomplish the task.
Delegating	The leader provides lower level of both relationship and task behavior, and is able to truly delegate tasks to team members.	Team members who are both skilled and motivated/confident in completing the task. *Note:* A mistake many leaders make is using this style with team members who require high direction or high relationship support. To delegate to a team member who is unskilled or lacks confidence in completing a task can hinder the team building process.

Activity—Leadership Styles and Team Members

Purpose

The purpose of this activity is to identify which leadership style is most appropriate for each of your team members. *N*ow even though you may not manage a team at work, you can complete this activity by thinking about a team you belong to, such as a sports team, a club team, or a family team.

Process

- Record the names of the members of your team.

- Identify and record the leadership style that you are currently using with each team member.

- Identify and record which leadership style you should be using with each team member.

- Explain what you need to do to improve your leadership style for each team member.

Team Member	Current Leadership Style	Appropriate Leadership Style	Steps to Change or Improve Leadership Style

Team Member Readiness

Situational Leadership defines readiness as the ability and willingness of a person to take responsibility for directing his or her own behavior. Readiness should be considered only in relation to a specific task or function that is going to be performed. People tend to have varying degrees of readiness depending on each task.

To determine what leadership style is appropriate in a given situation, first determine the readiness level of the team member in relation to a specific task. Consider the team member's ability and willingness to accomplish the task.

Ability: To consider the ability of a team member, consider the team member's knowledge, experience, or ability to direct his or her own behavior.

Willingness: To consider the willingness of a team member, consider the team member's confidence, commitment, and motivation used to direct his or her own behavior.

The Four Levels of Readiness

The four levels of readiness depend on the different combinations of ability and willingness that the team members bring to each task:

Level	Ability		Willingness
Readiness-1	low ability to perform the task	BUT	willing or confident in attempting the task
Readiness-2	low ability to perform the task	AND	has unwillingness or insecurity in performing the task
Readiness-3	strong ability to perform the task	BUT	has unwillingness or insecurity in performing the task
Readiness-4	strong ability to perform the task	AND	confidence in performing the task

Leadership Associated with Readiness

The leadership style you choose depends on the level of readiness of the team member.

If a team members has a(n)...	Then you must exhibit...
Low level of readiness	High task and low relationship behavior.
Increased level of readiness	Less task behavior and increased relationship behavior. Note: This is the case until the employee reaches a moderate level of readiness.
Above average level of readiness	A decrease of both task and relationship behavior. Ideally, the team member is ready to perform the task and is also confident and committed. For people at this level of readiness, a reduction of close supervision and an increase in delegation by the leader are positive indications of trust and confidence.

After reviewing the four different leadership styles and the four team member readiness levels, it is clear that the following readiness levels and leadership styles correspond:

- *Readiness Level 1 (R1) corresponds with the Directing style of leadership (S1)*
- *Readiness Level 2 (R2) corresponds with the Supporting style of leadership (S2)*
- *Readiness Level 3 (R3) corresponds with the Participating style of leadership (S3)*
- *Readiness Level 4 (R4) corresponds with the Delegating style of leadership (S4)*

This match of leadership style with team member readiness will produce the greatest chance for success in leading team members through task completion.

If the team member is...	Then use the...	And...
Unable to direct him- or herself but is willing and confident (R1)	Directing leadership style (high task and low relationship) (S1)	• Provide specific instructions • Supervise performance closely
Unable to direct him- or herself and is unwilling or insecure (R2)	Supporting leadership style (high task and high relationship) (S2)	• Explain decisions • Provide opportunity for clarification
Able to direct him- or herself but unwilling or insecure (R3)	Participating leadership style (low task and high relationship) (S3)	• Share ideas • Facilitate in decision-making
Able to direct him- or herself and is willing and confident (R4)	Delegating leadership style (low task and low relationship) (S4)	• Turn over responsibility for decisions and implementation

Valuing Diversity

Purpose

The purpose of this lesson is to help you understand and value diversity.

Objectives

Check each objective upon completion.

- ❑ Define diversity.

- ❑ Discuss the importance and consequences of diversity.

- ❑ Explain the sources of diversity.

- ❑ Describe each generation.

- ❑ Discuss how to value diversity.

Diversity

Diversity is defined as the condition of being different, point of difference, or variety[19].

Sources of Diversity

There is every reason to expect the diversity of individuals' cultural and experiential backgrounds, knowledge, abilities, and skills will continue to increase in the future.

The major sources of diversity are:

Diversity Source	Includes...	
Demographic	• culture • ethnicity • language • age • gender	• social class • religion • regional differences • handicapping conditions
Personality	• varying attitudes • values • lifestyles • commitments	• beliefs • opinions • styles of interaction • introversion / extroversion
Abilities and Skills	• varying experience • varying expertise	

Importance and Consequences of Diversity

Diversity among team members is a potential source of creativity and productivity. When you are in a leadership position, it is important that you identify the unique characteristics that each of your team members brings to the team. If you can effectively manage the diversity of your team, your team will be able to meet their goals. If you cannot manage the diversity of your team, you may experience some harmful consequences.

The following table lists the different consequences:

Beneficial Consequences	Harmful Consequences
Increased achievement and productivity	Discounting the importance of valuing the diversity amongst people includes the closed-minded rejection of new information
Creative problem solving	Increased egocentrism
Growth in cognitive and moral reasoning	Negative relationships characterized by hostility
Improved relationships	Rejection
Positive interaction with peers from different cultural and ethnic backgrounds	Divisiveness, stereotyping, prejudice, and racism

Generational Differences

As a leader in the 21st Century workplace, you are going to manage a very diverse team. One of the biggest challenges you will encounter is managing individuals from all of the different generations. How do you manage a generationally diverse team and keep them all motivated and productive?

- The first step is to explain to each generation what motivates the other generations.

- The second step is to establish practices that are flexible enough to meet each generation's needs.

Fundamental differences exist between those of different generations. You don't have to agree with what each generation values, but you do have to strive to understand the mind-sets of different generations in order to manage each generation.

Use the following pages that describe the different generations and their motivations and characteristics to answer the following questions:

Which generation do you belong to?

_____

_____

_____

What qualities would you add to your generation's description?

_____

_____

_____

Identify the generation of each of your team members.

Team Member	Generation

Traditionalists (Silent Generation, War Babies, Veterans)

Born before 1946

History:

The Great Depression, World War II influenced the Traditionalists' values.

Values:

- _Authority_: They have a lot of respect for authority.
- _Formality_: They prefer formal communication, whether written or oral, and formal dress.
- _Hard Work_: Their career identifies who they are so they believe in "paying their dues." They work hard because they feel that it is the right thing to do. (They may even get upset when others do not pay their dues.)
- _Privacy_: They are considered the silent generation because they will not share their inner thoughts.
- _Social Order_: They can be biased, prejudiced, racist or sexist.
- _Things_: They are sometimes referred to as "pack rats" because they do not get rid of their things; they believe that one day they may need them.
- _Trust_: They believe a leader's word is his or her bond.

Hints:

- Don't expect them to share their thoughts immediately; respect their privacy.
- Do what you say you'll do.
- Communicate in a formal manner, preferably face-to-face.
- Don't waste their time by not being prepared.

Baby Boomers (Boomers)

Born 1947 – 1965

History:

The Baby Boomers are the children of the Traditionalists, but they did not have to live through economic hard times because their parents protected them and wanted them to have a good life.

Values:

- *Anti-Rules & Regulations*: They don't appreciate rules for the sake of having rules, and they will challenge the system.
- *Body Language*: They are the "show me" generation and body language is important.
- *Change*: They like constant change.
- *Competition*: They value competition and can be seen by others as being egocentric.
- *Hard Work*: They were the first workaholics because it was necessary to work a lot to climb the corporate ladder.
- *Inclusion*: They will accept people on an equal basis as long as they can perform to their standards.
- *Success*: They are committed to climbing the ladder of success.
- *Teamwork*: They embrace a team-based approach to business—they are eager to get rid of the command-and-control style of their Traditionalist predecessors.
- *Will Fight For A Cause*: They don't like problems and have a history of fighting for causes.

Hints:

- Make sure your body language is appropriate when communicating.
- Be open and direct but avoid controlling language.
- Answer questions thoroughly.
- Present options to demonstrate flexibility.

Generation X (Xers)

Born 1966 - 1977

History:

Due to their parents' experiences of unemployment and double-digit inflation, Generation Xers are economically conservative and will not rely on institutions for their long-term security.

Values:

- *Entrepreneurial Spirit*: They invest in their own development rather than in their organization's development.
- *Feedback*: They need continuous positive and negative feedback. They use the feedback to adapt to new situations, because they are flexible.
- *Independence and Creativity*: They set clear goals for themselves and prefer to manage their own time and solve their own problems.
- *Information*: They value access to information and use plenty of it.
- *Quality of Work Life*: They work hard and find quicker and more efficient ways of working so they have time to balance work and personal responsibilities.

Hints:

- The primary communication tool is email.
- Be brief to keep their attention.
- Ask them for their feedback and provide them with regular feedback.
- Share information with them on a regular basis and strive to keep them in the loop.
- Use an informal communication style.

Generation Y (Nexters)

Born after 1977

History:

Generation Y grew up during the high-tech revolution; they have never known a world without high-speed video games, speed dial, and ATMs.

Values:

- _Positive Reinforcement_: They value constant positive reinforcement.
- _Autonomy_: They need independence.
- _Positive Attitudes_: They are optimistic because they grew up during good economic times.
- _Diversity_: They are used to diversity since they were exposed to it in their community or through the media.
- _Money_: They are used to making and spending money.
- _Technology_: They value technology and use it as a tool for multi-tasking.

Hints:

- Use action words.
- Challenge them at every opportunity.
- Do not talk down to them.
- They prefer email communication.
- Seek their feedback constantly and provide them with regular feedback.
- Use humor and create a fun work environment. Don't take yourself too seriously.
- Encourage them to take risks and break the rules so that they can explore new ways of doing things.

Valuing Diversity

Diversity cannot be avoided or ignored. Valuing diversity is a significant leadership strategy. It also is one of the major challenges facing managers today. However, dealing with diversity is increasingly important for several reasons:

- Changes in the world economy, transportation, and communication are resulting in increased levels of interdependence among individuals, groups, organizations, communities, and societies.

- It is only with the recent development of worldwide interdependent communication and transportation systems that diverse individuals have begun to interact, work with, and live next to each other.

- More and more organizations must translate their local and national perspectives into a worldview perspective as a result of the globalization of business.

What can you do to become more effective in managing and valuing diversity within your organization?

_____
_____
_____
_____
_____
_____
_____
_____
_____
_____
_____
_____
_____
_____
_____
_____
_____
_____
_____

If you can learn how to value, lead, and manage a diverse team you will succeed in your career.

Summary

To effectively lead your team you must complete the following:

- ❏ Understand the difference between management and leadership

- ❏ Apply motivational techniques to help others become self-motivated

- ❏ Understand the essentials of teamwork

- ❏ Implement team building activities

- ❏ Become a situational leader

- ❏ Value the diversity of each team member

Conclusion

You have successfully completed the YOUR STEPS TOWARD SUCCESS Career Resource Workbook. Your next step toward success is to apply the knowledge you have gained to choose your career, land the job you want, succeed in your career, and lead your team.

Your immediate next steps include:

- Sharing the information you have learned and encouraging others to obtain their own copy of the YOUR STEPS TOWARD SUCCESS Career Resource Workbook.

- Accessing the career resources available on Angela Dayton's websites at <www.YourStepsTowardSuccess.com> and <www.angeladayton.com>.

- Submitting your personal success stories to be published on the www.YourStepsTowardSuccess.com website.

Good luck and remember to refer to the YOUR STEPS TOWARD SUCCESS Career Resource Workbook throughout your career.

REFERENCES

For additional information, check the following resources:

Adams, Wendy, Suzanne Andrews, Jeff Brown, Marlene Bryan, Perri Capell, Max Carey, Jack Chapman, Don Doerr, Dave Edmonds, Phil Hey, Ed Holton, Keith Johnson, *Career Opportunity News.*

Aldag, Ramon J. and Timothy Stearns. *Management.* Cincinnati, OH: Southwestern Publishing, 1987.

Berry, Rick. *Observations On Generational Diversity.* Diversity Journal, May/June 2002.

Block, Peter. *The Empowered Manager.* San Francisco, CA: Jossey-Bass, 1987.

Denham, Thomas J. *Evaluating Job Offers & Negotiating Salary.*

E-Center for Business Ethics: <http://www.e-businessethics.com>

Fisher, Kimball. *Leading Self-Directed Work Teams: A Guide to Developing New Team Leadership Skills.* New York: McGraw-Hill, Inc., 1993.

Fisher, Roger, William Ury, and Bruce Patton. *Getting to Yes: Negotiating Agreement Without Giving In* (second edition). New York: Penguin Group Penguin Books USA Inc., 1991.

Gonyea, James C. *Electronic Résumés: Putting Your Résumé On-Line.* McGraw-Hill. 1996.

Gonyea, James C. *The On-Line Job Search Companion.* McGraw-Hill. 1994.

Hersey, Paul. *The Situational Leader.* San Diego, CA: University Associates, 1985.

Inc.com: <http://www.inc.com>

Johnson, David and Frank Johnson. *Joining Together.* A Pearson Company; Needham Heights, MA (2000).

Johnson, Keith. *Planning Job Choices: 1997.*

Katzenbach, John R. and Douglas K. Smith. *The Wisdom of Teams: Creating the High Performance Organization.* New York: HarperCollins., 1993.

Kennedy, Joyce Lian, Thomas J. Morrow. *Electronic Job Search Revolution.* John Wiley & Sons, Inc.

Kennedy, Joyce Lian, Thomas J. Morrow. *Hook Up, Get Hired.* John Wiley & Sons, Inc.

Kotter, John P. *Leading Change.* Boston, MA, Harvard Business School Press, 1996.

Krannich, Ronald L. and Carol Rae. *The New Network Your Way to Job and Career Success.* Impact Publications. 1992.

Newstrom, John W. *Games People Play.* New York, New York: McGraw Hill, 1980.

Oakley, Ed and Doug Krug. *Enlightened Leadership: Getting to the Heart of Change.* New York, New York: Simon and Schuster, 1991.

Odiorne, George S. *The Human Side of Management: Management by Integration and Self Control.* Lexington, MA: Lexington Books, 1987.

Riley, Margaret, Frances Roehm, and Steve Oserman. *The Guide to Internet Job Searching.* VGM Career Horizons.

Robbins, Stephen P. *Essentials of Organizational Behavior.* Upper Saddle River, NJ: Prentice-Hall, Inc, 2000.

Smith, Rebecca. *eRésumés & Resources.*

Snell, Alice. *The Job-Seeker's Guide to On-Line Resources.* Kennedy Publications.

Stewart, Thomas. *Planning a Career in a World Without Managers.* Fortune (March 20, 1995): 72-80.

Trainer's Workshop. *Employee Motivation: Empowering Your People to Excel.* American Management Association, December 1990.

Weddle, Peter D. *Electronic Résumés for the New Job Market: Résumés That Work for You 24 Hours a Day, Seven Days a Week.* Impact Publications.

Weisbord, Marvin R. Productive Workplaces: Organizing and Managing for Dignity, Meaning, and Community. San Francisco, CA: Jossey-Bass, 1991.

ACTIVITY KEY-TOP TEN QUALITIES DEFINED

Activity— Define The Top Ten Qualities

The following table defines each quality:

Quality	Definition
Communication Skills (verbal and written)	The exchange of thoughts, messages, or information, using speech, signals, writing or behavior. The art and technique of using words effectively to convey information or ideas.
Honesty/Integrity	Truthfulness and steadfast adherence to a strict moral or ethical code.
Teamwork Skills	Cooperative effort by the members of a group or team to achieve a common goal.
Strong Work Ethic	Set of values based on moral virtues of hard work and diligence.
Analytical Skills	Able to analyze. Dividing into elemental parts or basic principles. Reasoning or acting from a perception of the parts and interrelations of a subject.
Flexibility/Adaptability	Responsive to change or adaptable.
Interpersonal Skills	Positive interactions between individuals.
Motivation/Initiative	The psychological feature that encourages action toward a desired goal. The power or ability to begin or to follow through energetically with a plan or task.
Computer Skills	Familiar with basic computer applications, word processing, etc.
Detail-oriented	Attention to specifics.

Sources: Webster's Dictionary and Dictionary.com

ACTIVITY KEY-MANAGEMENT VERSUS LEADERSHIP

Activity—Distinguish Between Leadership and Management Characteristics

The following table outlines some of the different characteristics between leadership and management:

Leadership	Management
Motivates Others	Directs Others
Inspires Others	Focuses on the Process
Creates a Vision	Focuses on the Bottom Line
Asks Questions	Follows Orders
Uses Creativity	Uses Formal Solutions
Identifies Opportunities	Maintains Current Responsibilities
Takes Risks	Takes Few Risks
Manages Change	Likes Control
Sets Goals	Achieves Goals

ENDNOTES

[1] *Biotechnology Industry Organization.* Retrieved October 2005 from <www.bio.org>

[2] *U.S. Bureau of Labor Statistics (BLS), National Employment Data.* Retrieved October 2005 from <www.bls.gov/emp/home.htm#data> Occupation search for "biological"

[3] U.S. Department of Commerce, "A Survey of the Use of Biotechnology in U.S. Industry," Executive Summary for the Report to Congress.

[4] *Industry Workstation, Biotech Industry Forecast.* Retrieved October 2005 from Economy.com.

[5] BLS, Jay Berman, "Industry output and employment projections to 2012," Monthly Labor Review, February 2004, p. 63.

[6] *BLS, National Employment Data.* Retrieved October 2005 from <www.bls.gov/emp/home.htm#data> Occupation search for "biological."

[7] *U.S. Department of Commerce.* Retrieved October 2005 from <www.technology.gov/reports/Biotechnology/ CD120a_0310.pdf> p. 88.

[8] *Career InfoNet.* Retrieved March 2006 from <http://www.careerinfonet.org/acinet/ occ_rep.asp?next=occ_rep&level=&optstatus=000 00000&stfips=&jobfam=&id=1& nodeid=2&keyword=BIOLOGICAL+TECHNICIAN&soccode=194021&x=53&y=14>

[9] *Webster's Dictionary.* Retrieved March 2006 from <http://www.webster.com/dictionary/ethics>

[10] Do the Right Thing (Training and Development Magazine July 2001.)

[11] ibid.

[12] Fandray, Dayton: <u>Workforce</u>, December 2000.

[13] *Fredick Herzberg.* Retrieved March 2006 from <http://www.accelteam.com/human_relations/hrels_05_herzberg.html>

[14] *David C. McClelland.* Retrieved March 2006 from <http://www.accelteam.com/human_relations/hrels_06_mcclelland.html>

[15] *ERG Theory-Clayton P. Alderfer.* Retrieved March 2006 from <http://www.valuebasedmanagement.net/methods_alderfer_erg_theory.html>

[16] *Maslow's Hierarchy of Needs.* Retrieved March 2006 from <http://en.wikipedia.org/wiki/Self-actualization>

[17] Katzenbach, J.R. and Smith, D.K. The Wisdom of Teams: Creating the High Performance Organization. New York: HarperCollins, 1993.

[18] *Bruce Tuckman's 1965 Team-Development Model.* Retrieved March 2006 from <http://www.businessballs.com/tuckmanformingstormingnormingperforming.htm>

[19] *Webster's Dictionary.* Retrieved March 2006 from <http://www.webster.com/dictionary/Diversity>

ABOUT THE AUTHOR

Angela Dayton has first-hand knowledge of the skills and competencies that American businesses are looking for in the future workforce. She gained this knowledge by meeting with over 2,000 industry leaders (Chief Executive Officers, Senior Vice Presidents, and Human Resource Directors) of small, medium, and large corporations, such as Hospital Corporation of America, Marriott, Astrazeneca, Gore, Inc., BMW, Snap-On Tools, Bank of America, Shell Oil, Industrial Precision Components Corp., IBM, etc. She has also worked with industry associations like the National Association of Manufacturers, the National Restaurant Association, the National Retail Foundation, the Automotive Youth Educational Foundation, the Financial Industry Roundtable, CompTIA, and many others.

Angela has helped identify and develop solutions for the critical workforce challenges facing American businesses. Her knowledge and expertise in the YOUR STEPS TOWARD SUCCESS Career Resource Workbook will offer new insights and prepare any student or job seeker who is ready to tackle the hottest careers of the future.

Angela has ten years of training and development experience. She served as the Coordinator for President George W. Bush's High Growth Job Training Initiative, a Senior Instructional Designer for the U.S. Department of Labor, a Training and Communications Project Manager for Morgan Stanley, an Independent Facilitator for Franklin Covey, a Trainer for Delta Air Lines, and was the National Western Region Vice President for the college division of DECA. Angela has also started and operated two small businesses – AP Management and Dayton Consulting.

Angela holds a Master of Science degree in Instructional Technology from Utah State University and a Bachelors of Science degree in Technical Sales from Weber State University. She has been a member of the American Society for Training and Development, the International Society for Performance Improvement, DECA, an Association of Marketing Students, and Future Business Leaders of America.

The phrase "Step Toward Success" represents Angela Dayton, and now she is sharing her expertise and knowledge through the YOUR STEPS TOWARD SUCCESS Career Resource Workbook, Facilitator Guide, and seminar presentations.

George W. Bush, President of the United States of America and Angela Dayton, Coordinator for President George W. Bush's High Growth Job Training Initiative

Elaine Chao, Secretary, U.S. Department of Labor and Angela Dayton, Coordinator for President George W. Bush's High Growth Job Training Initiative

www.YourStepsTowardSuccess.com   *www.AngelaDayton.com*

Envision yourself with a successful career. You are influential, effective, and respected. How can you progress from being one of the many students on the congested thoroughfares of commerce to becoming a successful leader with boundless opportunities to impact organizations?

You must gain the knowledge necessary to help you move forward in your career. Knowledge is power, and through the *Your Steps Toward Success* Career Resource Workbook you will learn how to achieve success in your career by increasing your career knowledge, developing your leadership skills, and improving your ability to communicate.

Choosing Your Career
The first step toward success is choosing the career that is right for you. This series of lessons will assist you in selecting an occupation by instructing you to conduct a self-analysis, research occupations in high growth industries, develop a training and education plan, and set professional goals.

Landing The Job You Want
Landing the job you want is the key to starting a successful career. You must secure employment before you can succeed. This series of lessons enhances your knowledge about searching for the right job, networking effectively, writing a winning résumé and cover letter, developing a career portfolio, understanding interview strategies, negotiating salary and benefits, and ultimately selecting the best job offer.

Advancing In Your Career
If you want to reach the next level in your career, then you must display certain qualities in your everyday professional life. This series of lessons focus on the qualities you must have to climb the career ladder. You will learn how to make a good impression, become an effective communicator, and how to handle ethical dilemmas. Once you have mastered these basic skills, you will have the skills necessary to advance in your career.

Leading Your Team To Success
Now that you have landed your chosen job and advanced up the career ladder, the next step is to effectively lead your team. To be a successful leader you must possess and understand the knowledge and skills that are necessary to influence and manage your team. In this series of lessons you will learn the difference between management and leadership, components of motivation, foundations of teamwork, and the value of diversity. Once you have become an effective leader, you will be an influential manager with a productive team, which will ultimately make you successful in your career.

Share the news about the *Your Steps Toward Success* Career Resource Workbook Today!

The YOUR STEPS TOWARD SUCCESS Career Resource Workbook can be used as an independent learning tool for students and job seekers, or it can be used as a curriculum when instructors use the YOUR STEPS TOWARD SUCCESS Facilitator Guide.

The YOUR STEPS TOWARD SUCCESS Facilitator Guide contains all of the tools instructors need to successfully facilitate the YOUR STEPS TOWARD SUCCESS workbook curriculum.

The YOUR STEPS TOWARD SUCCESS Facilitator Guide creates an interactive learning environment for the participants by providing instructors with the following tools:

- Detailed Instructions
- Presentation Materials
- Talking Points
- Activities

- Examples
- Role-Play Scripts
- Videos
- Answer Keys

As instructors use the YOUR STEPS TOWARD SUCCESS Facilitator Guide, participants will feel involved and confident in taking their first steps toward success.

Printed in the United States
78755LV00001B/85-96